DON BOSCO

MICHAEL T WINSTANLEY SDB

DON BOSCO

Don Bosco Publications
Thornleigh House, Sharples Park

Bolton
BL1 6PQ
www.don-bosco-publications.co.uk
01204 308811

New Revised Standard Version of the Bible: Anglicised Edition, copyright 1989,
1995, Division of Christian Education of the National Council of the Churches
of Christ in the United States of America. Used by permission.
All rights reserved.

New Jerusalem Bible published and copyright 1966, 1967, 1968 and 1974 by
Darton, Longman and Todd Ltd, and used by permission of the publishers.

Permission has been sought for all quotations in this book.

© Michael T Winstanley
© Front Cover Illustration Sharon Hulme

Other books by M. T. Winstanley SDB
Come and See (London, DLT 1985)
Into Your Hands (Homebush, St Pauls 1994)
Scripture, Sacraments, Spirituality (Great Wakering, McCrimmons 2002)

ISBN 0-9538991-9-5
© Don Bosco Publications
Thornleigh House
Bolton BL1 6PQ
Tel 01204 308 811

Printed by Printoff Graphic Arts Ltd

INTRODUCTION

I am very fond of music. For many years I have been fascinated by the variety of ways in which individual artists, groups, bands, and orchestras develop their own distinctive style and sound. The same tune, aria, or orchestral score is open to widely different interpretations. One can compare the Westlife or Abba versions of *I have a dream*, the Pavarotti, Bocelli or Watson renderings of *Nessun Dorma*, the Menuhin or Kennedy performances of Mendelssohn or Bruch violin concertos, the Liverpool and Birmingham Phil's execution of the great symphonies. It is also interesting to observe how different people seem drawn to particular interpretations, as evidenced in T shirt culture and the plethora of fan clubs.

Something analogous is true when we consider the Gospel of Jesus. Over the centuries Christians have responded to the Gospel in a rich variety of ways. Some individuals have felt drawn by the Spirit to emphasise particular aspects of Jesus' life, message and challenge. They have fashioned their own distinctive interpretation and response, their distinctive style and *sound*. Such figures include Benedict, Francis of Assisi and Clare, Dominic, Ignatius, John of the Cross and Teresa of Avila. Other Christians have subsequently felt drawn to the styles of Gospel living to which these inspired individuals have given birth, and great traditions of spirituality have developed in the Christian community, traditions which are very much alive today.

In the Piedmont of the mid-nineteenth century a young priest called Don Bosco was drawn to the spirituality of St Francis of Sales, the famous Bishop of Geneva. He named the religious order which he founded, the Salesians, after him. He adapted salient traits of his spirituality as he fashioned his own distinctive way of following the Gospel, and his particular mission to young people. This book is an attempt to explore some of the scriptural background which underpins Don Bosco's Gospel Way.

On a number of occasions I have led retreats for the Salesian Family. For two spells I have been a lecturer in New Testament studies at Ushaw College. In preparing my retreats I have sought to use the insights made available by modern biblical scholarship. This book is the outcome of both these aspects of my life. I am convinced that Don Bosco's way of Christian discipleship, the system of attitudes and values which he espoused, his vision and his style of ministry, are deeply rooted in the Gospel of Jesus. I am excited by this, and I wish to share my enthusiasm with others in the Salesian Family, and with all interested people.

In the first two chapters I explore our understanding of God and its implications for our lives. I then look at two aspects of the Gospel portrayal of Jesus, his compassion and his role as shepherd. Next I look at aspects of our response to Jesus: relationship, reverence and the call to be both contemplative and active. Finally, I examine ways in which we can articulate our sharing in the mission of Jesus, and I conclude with a study of the Emmaus story, a narrative which touches upon many facets of our life experience and our ministries. Two other important aspects of Don Bosco's way, the sacraments of Reconciliation and Eucharist, I have chosen to omit because I have recently presented the scriptural background to these sacraments in a separate publication. At the end of each chapter there are suggestions for prayer and further reflection.

My love of the scriptures has been nourished over the years by the work of many scholars. I wish to express my thanks to them. In the notes, which I have sought to keep to a minimum, I have tried to acknowledge the authors on whom I have depended most, and I apologise in advance for any omissions which may have occurred. My love of Don Bosco has been stimulated and enriched by countless members of the Salesian Family who have touched my life. To these I am profoundly grateful. I would like to thank Fr George Chalissery, whose kind invitation to preach to my confreres in East Africa in June/July provided the occasion and stimulus for rewriting the material in these pages.

This year the community at Savio House, to which I belong, is celebrating fifty years of Salesian work. I therefore dedicate this book to all those people – Salesian priests, brothers, sisters and cooperators, lay women and men, volunteers and staff, families and friends – who have shared our life and our mission to the young over this half century. I do so in the hope and with a prayer that readers may deepen their understanding and appreciation of Don Bosco's way of living the Gospel, especially in the service of young people.

Michael T Winstanley, SDB
Savio House
Bollington.
September 29th 2002

WHO WAS DON BOSCO?

John Bosco was an Italian Catholic priest. In Italy priests are often called *Don* as a title similar to the use of *Father* in English-speaking countries. He worked in Turin during the nineteenth century and founded a religious family called the Salesians. His impact on educational practice was immense. He began on the streets of Turin, with the poorest street children, and developed a way of dealing with them which he enshrined in his *Preventive System*. This was rooted in *presence*, walking with young people as a friend, who becomes a leader.

His principles ring true today as they did in the nineteenth century. They are based on his experience of success with the abandoned young people of his day. A principle such as, *it is not sufficient to love young people, they must know they are loved*, is as obvious as it is difficult. In the mind of Don Bosco the word *preventive* is far richer than merely *preventative*. It means the ability to be one step ahead of young people, reading their needs before they became aware of them, and being there to give them the encouragement to succeed.

Don Bosco gathered young people into what he called an *Oratory*. The Oratory was more than a place of prayer. It became for so many young people a school, a church, a playground and a home. The vital part of this fourfold provision was balance. No young person was pushed to pursue one at the expense of the other. Don Bosco's system is more than a nineteenth century insight. It is a living tradition, refined year by year by the Salesian Family, which he established. It has flourished in a remarkable way for over 100 years in more than 100 countries throughout the world.

CHAPTER ONE- THE GOD OF LUKE

An excellent way to begin our reflections on Don Bosco's Gospel Way is to take a look at the Infancy Narrative in Luke's Gospel. At first sight this may seem strange, since we tend naturally to link this part of the Gospel with the celebration of Christmas. However, the narrative is obviously written from an Easter and Pentecost perspective. Many scenes from the Infancy Narrative are, in fact, proposed for our reflection from time to time in the course of the liturgical year. This occurs, for example, on the feasts of the Annunciation, the Visitation, and the Birth of John the Baptist. We are probably quite familiar with them. I suspect, however, that we rarely read the narrative as a whole, and so its cumulative impact may be missed. The narrative is really all about the presence and action of God. It proclaims an understanding of God, which should be the foundation of Salesian Spirituality. I propose to highlight for our reflection three aspects of the God revealed through Luke's storytelling.[1]

GOD, FREE AND FAITHFUL IN LOVE

The first impression, which a reading of Luke's narrative leaves with me, is a profound sense of God's freedom and initiative. At the outset God intervenes in the story of the elderly couple Elizabeth and Zechariah, enabling them to have their longed-for child despite their advancing years and Elizabeth's barrenness. It is God who, through his angel, gives the child a name and spells out his future Elijah-like role.[2] What God promises is later fulfilled in the conception, birth, and naming of John, later known as the Baptist.

God intervenes even more dramatically in the life of Mary, the young maiden of Nazareth, who is betrothed to Joseph, of the House of David. God favours her in an unprecedented manner. Through the overshadowing of the Spirit she becomes the mother of a child, who would be called Son of the Most High. In parallel fashion God indicates through Gabriel the child's personal name, Jesus, and goes on to inform Mary of her relative's startling pregnancy. Later, when this child is born in Bethlehem, the city of David, it is God who through his angels reveals to the shepherds in the countryside the good news of the child's birth

---

[1] I have found the following commentaries on Luke's Gospel very useful: G C Caird, *St Luke* (London, Pelican 1963); E E Ellis, *The Gospel of Luke* (London, Oliphants 1974); C F Evans, *Saint Luke* (London, SCM 1990); J A Fitzmyer, *The Gospel according to Luke* (New York, Doubleday, vol 1 1981, vol 2 1985); L T Johnson, *The Gospel of Luke* (Collegeville, The Liturgical Press 1991); I H Marshall, *The Gospel of Luke* (Exeter, Paternoster Press 1978); D McBride, *The Gospel of Luke* (Dublin, Dominican Publications 1991).
[2] Luke 1:5-25

and identity. They are encouraged to go to find him, swaddled and lying in a manger.[3]

This God is indeed the God of surprises, the God of the unexpected, a God who cannot be predicted or controlled, a God who is supremely and disconcertingly free, a God who is God. God's action in our story is also consonant with what has been revealed and understood about God in the Old Testament:

Yahweh, God of tenderness and compassion, slow to anger, rich in faithful love and constancy. (Exod.34:6)[4]

The narrative is resonant with echoes of other people, Abraham and Sarah, Hannah and Elkinah. They have all experienced both the unexpected and transforming intervention, and the tender, faithful love of Israel's God. As the story unfolds, Elizabeth, on realising that she has at last conceived a child, recognises with joy and gratitude that:

The Lord has done this for me, now that it has pleased him to take away the humiliation I suffered in public. (Luke 1:25)

When eventually the child is born, her neighbours and relatives share her rejoicing. They acknowledge that *the Lord had lavished on her his faithful love*.[5] In popular etymology, the name which God had decreed should be given to the child, John, means *God is gracious*.

The two beautiful hymns of the Infancy Narrative, with which we are very familiar, continue this theme. In the *Magnificat* Mary celebrates God as Saviour, who has looked upon the lowliness of his servant. She praises God because *his faithful love extends age after age to those who fear him*.[6] In the concluding summary of that hymn she sings: *He has come to the help of Israel his servant, mindful of his faithful love - according to the promise he made to our ancestors - of his mercy to Abraham and his descendants for ever.* She recognises that what is happening to her, and through her, is an expression of God's faithfulness and compassionate love, reaching out to help and to save. This is in line with a long history of such love and faithfulness, right back to the time of Abraham.

---

3 Lk 2:1-20
4 See Psalm 103:8; 86:15; 145:8-9; Ecclus 2:11. All the scripture references in this chapter are NJB.
5 1:58
6 Lk 1:50

In the *Benedictus* too Zechariah places the birth of his child in the same context of God's promises *from ancient times*, God's *faithful love to our ancestors*. God's *keeping in mind his holy covenant*, again specifically referring to Abraham. At the end of the hymn, when the future Messiah is referred to, Zechariah again mentions the *faithful love of our God*,[7] which has given rise to this saving *visitation*. In the Jerusalem Temple, Simeon too, as he holds the child Jesus in his arms, recognises with gratitude that God has been faithful to the promise made him. Now he is ready to depart in peace and contentment.

A SAVING GOD

The idea of God visiting his people is mentioned twice in the *Benedictus*. As is so often the case in the Old Testament, such a visit takes place for the purpose of liberating and saving. Zechariah is told by Gabriel that his future child *will bring back many of the Israelites to the Lord their God*,[8] and that, following in the footsteps of Elijah as extolled by the prophet Micah, he will have a reconciling role.[9] The child to be born of Mary is to be named Jesus, which was held to mean *God saves*. Mary praises God, as Saviour, in the *Magnificat*. She describes this salvation as including the reversing of many of the unjust and painful situations in society, in favour of the poor and lowly ones. The *Benedictus* speaks about God's establishing a *saving power* or *horn of salvation* in the House of David, and refers to God's promise to save the people from their enemies,[10] and *deliver* them from the hands of their foes.[11] The role of the future Baptist is described as *to give his people knowledge of salvation through the forgiveness of their sins*.[12] This knowledge is not theoretical, head knowledge, but based on experience.

In Luke's well known presentation of the birth of Jesus in the Bethlehem stable, the heart of the episode consists in God's revealing to the shepherds the good news that will bring such joy to them and to the whole people:

> **Today in the town of David a Saviour has been born to you; he is Christ the Lord.** (2:11)

[7] 1:78
[8] 1:16
[9] 1:17
[10] 1:71
[11] 1:74
[12] 1:77

This, I believe, is the central message or proclamation of the entire Infancy Narrative. This child is the consummate expression of God's saving love; his mission in life is to bring about our salvation. This announcement gives greater significance to the later statement that after eight days *they gave him the name Jesus, the name the angel had given him before his conception.*[13]

This motif is taken up in the subsequent scene, when Simeon comes to the Temple and receives the child in his arms. He blesses God for God's faithfulness in bringing his own and his nation's hopes to fulfilment. He proclaims that he is happy to die, *for my eyes have seen the salvation which you have made ready* - a salvation which is not limited to Israel, but will extend to all the nations.[14] Also the prophetess Anna, still alert and sensitive in her old age, praises God and speaks about the child *to all who looked forward to the deliverance of Jerusalem.*[15]

When taken together in the different scenes of the infancy drama, these various expressions communicate an intensely powerful understanding of God as Saviour.

THE HOLY SPIRIT

Another salient characteristic of Luke's presentation of God in the Infancy Narrative is the activity of the Spirit. At the beginning of the story Gabriel informs Zechariah that the child to be born to the aged couple *even from his mother's womb will be filled with the Holy Spirit.*[16] In the case of Mary, she is told by the angel that *the Holy Spirit will come upon you, and the power of the Most High will cover you with its shadow.*[17] These images recall the description of God's presence at the dawn of creation; a new creation is now taking place. It is through the presence and power of the Spirit that she will conceive, and that her child will be called Holy and Son of God. Later, when she reaches the hill-country home of Zechariah and Elizabeth and greets her kinswoman, we are informed that *Elizabeth was filled with the Holy Spirit.*[18] She becomes aware of what is happening in Mary - her blessedness as the mother of the Lord. After the birth of John the Baptist, and the debate about his name, Zechariah insists that he be called John, at which his power of speech returns, and he too *was filled with the Holy Spirit* and was led to prophecy in the words of the *Benedictus.*[19]

[13] 2:21   [17] 1:35
[14] 2:32   [18] 1:41
[15] 2:38   [19] 1:67
[16] 1:15

Finally, the presence of the Spirit is very much in evidence when Jesus is presented in the Temple, forty days after his birth. Simeon is described as upright and devout; *and the Spirit rested upon him*,[20] a lovely phrase. Through the Spirit it has been revealed to him that he will not die before setting eyes on the Messiah. It is through the Spirit's prompting that he comes to the Temple that day. I think that we are meant to understand that it is through the Spirit that he recognises the identity and significance of the child. This is expressed in the terms of the canticle *Nunc Dimittis*:

a light of revelation for the gentiles and glory for your people Israel. (2:32)

Though the Spirit is not specifically mentioned with regard to Anna, who comes into the scene at that point, her piety, prophetic gifts and praise are an indication of the Spirit's presence in her life.

CONCLUSION

These first two chapters of Luke, through which he launches his Gospel and the Book of Acts, provide us with an interpretative key with which we can approach his proclamation of the Good News. Behind the unfolding story of Jesus of Nazareth and subsequently of the early Christian community, is to be found this God of tenderness and compassion. A God who is rich in faithful love and constancy, a God of surprises, creative and free. In Jesus, God breaks decisively into our human history in order to save our world. God pours out the Spirit to reveal and enlighten, to transform and touch into life, to empower. This same God, we believe, is behind our own stories in the making, behind the stories of our families and communities, breaking through into our lives, enabling new and unexpected things to happen.

The Salesian Constitutions read in the context of our reflection on Luke's Infancy Narrative, takes on a deeper significance. They state that the Salesian Congregation *came into being not as a merely human venture but by the initiative of God*.[21] It is the same God who is behind the Salesian story too. The Salesian way of life or spirituality is the result of God's free and faithful love, breaking once more into human history. It is another element in the unfolding of God's plan, the history of salvation.

12

---

[20] 2:25
[21] Constitution 1 (All the italics in the conclusion are from this constitution.)

The creative, dynamic, life-giving activity of the Spirit is at work: the Holy Spirit raised up St John Bosco to contribute to the salvation of youth. The Spirit formed within him the heart of a father and teacher. To ensure the continuation of this mission, the Spirit inspired him to initiate various apostolic projects, first among them the Salesian Congregation. From this active presence of the Holy Spirit we draw strength for our fidelity and support for our hope. This is an unusually powerful emphasis on the Spirit's role in the coming to birth and growth of the Salesian experience.

The objective of God's *visitation*, God's calling and sending of Don Bosco, is *the salvation of youth*. Don Bosco shares the saving and life-giving mission of Jesus; he focuses particularly on extending that salvation to young people. Don Bosco spoke so often about the salvation of souls, salvation understood in a holistic sense. That was how he articulated his life's work, what he was about. Mary, who is such a central figure in Luke's Infancy story, was a motherly presence in Don Bosco's story, and continues to be such a presence throughout the Salesian story.

PRAYER SUGGESTION
Perhaps we could look back at our lives and recall occasions when we believe God has broken into our lives and surprised us, touched us with His faithful love. We could also reflect on our ongoing need for salvation, for the liberation and new life which Jesus continues to offer. We could look at our wider world and highlight situations which clamour for salvation, particularly situations which threaten the young. We could reflect on our sensitivity to the presence of the Spirit in our lives, as the One who enlightens, enlivens and empowers.

CHAPTER TWO - A SEARCHING GOD

In this second chapter I would like to continue to explore our understanding of God, the God behind the Salesian mission and spirituality. I propose to stay with Luke's Gospel, and to begin with a typical scene in the ministry of Jesus.[1]

TABLE FELLOWSHIP

> Now all the tax collectors and sinners were coming near to listen to him. And the Pharisees and the scribes were grumbling and saying, 'This fellow welcomes sinners and eats with them.' (15: 1-2)

The marginalised and religious outcasts, in large numbers, are drawing close to Jesus. Their purpose is to listen to him. This, for Luke, is an indication of an openness to conversion. In the background are the religious elite, the *Pharisees and scribes*. They keep their distance to avoid contamination. They shun table fellowship with sinners. They *grumble* repeatedly and openly. Their criticism is focused not only on Jesus eating and drinking with these people, as on earlier occasions in the narrative,[2] but also on his welcoming them, his offering them hospitality. To host or entertain sinners was a more serious offence to the scribes and Pharisees than simply to eat with sinners informally or to accept invitations, which was itself scandalous enough.

In that culture to share table was a very significant gesture. It was a sign of acceptance, respect and trust, an offer of peace, brotherhood and friendship. To share table indicated a being *at home* with the other, a willingness to share life, an identification and oneness with them; it was an expression of solidarity. Jesus' action bridged the social and religious divide in a culture extremely conscious of status, class, and prestige. It showed the sinners and outcasts that they mattered to him, that they had a value. It was a healing and liberating event. Since Jesus was looked upon as in some way a man of God, a prophet, his gesture of friendship communicated and experienced through table fellowship, would have been understood as an indication of God's approval and forgiveness. Through the welcome he extended, *he was declaring on his own authority that anyone who trusted in him and his kingdom-announcement was*

---

[1] On the parables in Luke's Gospel I have found the following particularly enriching: K E Bailey, *Poet & Peasant, and Through Peasant Eyes* (Grand Rapids, Eerdmans, 1984) and J R Donahue, *The Gospel in Parable* (Philadelphia, Fortress 1988). See also M T Winstanley, *Scripture, Sacraments, Spirituality* (McCrimmons, Great Wakering 2002), p 80-83; *Come and See* (London, DLT 1985), p 23-26.

[2] 5:30; see 7:34

within the Kingdom.[3] This gesture is the most powerful parable of the Kingdom; it proclaims the message and makes present the reality of God's nearness in saving love.

The great scripture scholar Jeremias writes that, *the inclusion of sinners in the community of salvation, achieved in table fellowship, is the most meaningful expression of the message of the redeeming love of God.*[4] I believe that we can affirm that this symbolic gesture contains the whole Gospel, the Good News, in a nutshell.

THE TWIN PARABLES

In Luke's narrative the response of Jesus to the criticism of the Pharisees is to explain his attitude and conduct by recounting three parables. There are two short parables presented in parallel and carefully matched: the parables of the lost sheep and the lost coin. Then there is the longer and very familiar parable of the two lost sons, normally and misleadingly referred to as the parable of the prodigal son. In fact, I think that the usual emphasis on loss in these parables is misplaced. In the Lukan context I prefer to see them as parables of seeking and finding that which is lost. The seeking is demanding and costly. The finding calls for joyful celebration.

The twin parables reflect Luke's typical interest in equal opportunities. There are male and female protagonists. The parables build on our human experience of losing things which are important to us. The great efforts of finding them is balanced by the joy and satisfaction of discovery. You may like to recall for a moment a recent experience of this. Jesus is saying that God is no less persistent in seeking nor less jubilant in finding. God sets a high value on the lost, and spares no effort to recover it. One aspect which I find fascinating here is that Jesus chooses, as pointers to the depths of God's being, a shepherd and a woman. To tend sheep was a low-class occupation, a role avoided by religious people; it was one of the proscribed trades; one carrying it out would be considered a *sinner* by the religious elite. Women in that cultural milieu suffered religious and social discrimination, and had very little value. So Jesus is being creative and quite provocative. Parables are meant to make people sit up and take notice. Another significant point is the fact that the sheep and the coin don't do anything; the seeking and the finding are gift. For Jesus the emphasis is not on conversion, but on God's gratuitous searching love.

3 N T Wright, *Jesus and the Victory of God* (London, SPCK 1996), p 274.
4 J Jeremias, *New Testament Theology* (London, SCM 1971), p 116.

So Jesus bases his ministry on his understanding of the mind and heart of God. He takes his cue from that knowledge. His table fellowship is his way of articulating his mission. It is revelation of God and of God's purpose.

A FATHER SEARCHING FOR LOST SONS

The classic longer parable which brings the trilogy to a climax is probably the best known and loved of all Jesus' parables. Both sons are lost. One in a foreign pig-sty, far from home. The other at home on the farm. The parable tells of the extravagant, almost prodigal, love of the father, as he searches for them both. The younger he finds, and there is a celebration. The older? We are left to ponder.

The story is very familiar, but I believe that it is well worth revisiting. The retreat house where I live has a long, tree-lined drive. I frequently take a brisk walk down to the end and back. It is never quite the same. There is always something new to be noticed – maybe because of the light or the season, or maybe because of how I am feeling. This is also true, I believe, with the words of scripture. Even passages which we know well can surprise us.

In the culture of Jesus, any transfer of the ownership of property usually took place after the father's death. There are some instances where a father divided his property before his death, despite the cautions against such a course of action found in Sirach.[5] It was unheard of for a son to ask for it. The younger son's request is tantamount to wishing for his father's death, and is an extraordinary insult. In granting the request, the father demonstrates enormous love for his son.

The young man must have made a further request to dispose of his share, and this request too was granted. Having quickly realised his assets, he wastes no time in leaving. He leaves home, rejecting all that it stands for. He is prepared to sever his relationship with his father, showing no regard for his feelings or future well-being. Leaving his brother does not pose a problem; they do not seem to be particularly close. The elder brother apparently makes no attempt to mediate, to reconcile, as was expected in that culture. Without protest, he benefits from the transaction, since the father *divided the estate between them*. The closely knit village community would have been horrified at what had happened.

5 33:20-24

The young man sets off for a foreign country. This was not uncommon at the time, given the precarious nature of the Palestinian agrarian economy. There he squandered his money on a life of pleasure and extravagance. The situation changes dramatically with the onset of famine. Penniless and friendless, he is obliged to hire himself out to a Gentile landowner, who sends him to tend the pigs. As a Jew, he is thus totally alienated, the epitome of being lost. And he is starving to death. His hunger galvanises him into action. He makes a snap decision to return home, where his father's *hired men have all the food they want*. He is prepared to acknowledge that he has done wrong, and plans to ask his father to take him on as a hired servant. This would enable him to maintain his independence and social respectability, living in the village. And he could use his income to fulfil the financial responsibilities to his father which he had selfishly abandoned. He seems to wish to return on his own terms, to do things his way.

The spotlight switches and focuses on the father. The key to the whole parable is found in the description of the father's response when he catches sight of the returning younger son in the distance:

> **So he set off and went to his father. But while he was still far off, his father saw him and was filled with compassion; he ran and put his arms around him and kissed him.** (15:20 NRS)

All that follows in the narrative springs from compassion. The father runs to meet his son. Normally an elder would not run; it was socially unacceptable. But it enables him to meet the young man outside the village boundary and protect him from the inevitable hostility of the villagers, outraged by the whole saga. A remarkable reconciliation takes place. The father says nothing; there is no lecture or blame or criticism. His actions express his profound love, acceptance and welcome. He kisses him repeatedly in a firm embrace, a sign of forgiveness, a recognising that he is his son. This is public, for all the villagers to see. None of them will cause him harassment now.

The son forgets the crippling hunger which prompted his decision to return. He abandons his plan of maintaining his independence as a hired servant. He comes to realise that what is at issue is a broken relationship, a relationship which he cannot heal. The possibility of that relationship being re-established can only come as a pure gift from his father. He perceives, from his father's behaviour, that such an offer is being made. The robe, signet ring, and shoes are symbols of this. The father's compassionate love brings about a change within him. He graciously accepts the gift freely and generously offered, beyond his wildest dreams. The father sets in motion the arrangements for a great celebration. The whole village community would be invited so as to participate in their rejoicing, and share in the restoration and reconciliation which has occurred. The father sums up his view of things:

> **for this son of mine was dead and is alive again; he was lost and is found!** (15:24)

To the *lost and found* language of the two shorter parables is added the image of death and resurrection.

The other son returns from the fields and becomes aware of the party, for there is music in the air. He plies one of the local children with questions. The youngster, without guile, informs him that his brother has returned home and that his father has killed the fatted calf to celebrate. The older brother reacts angrily and refuses to participate in the meal which has been prepared. He remains outside, refusing to join in the fun, and unwilling to fulfil his role as master of ceremonies. This is a public insult to his father. The father reacts by coming out of the house and pleading with him. He comes in search of his older son. The latter's response reveals the extent of his alienation. There is no respect, no affection; he complains bitterly, betraying the attitude of a slave rather than a son. He is self-righteous about his impeccable obedience, disparagingly critical of his father's other son whom he refuses to acknowledge as his brother. Obviously, he is quite incapable of understanding and entering into his father's joy. From the father there is no outburst of anger, no criticism, no recall to duty. Rather, he reaches out with love and compassion, searching to bridge the gulf between them – *My son, you are with me always and all I have is yours.*

He reassures him that his rights are still secure and protected, and finally reminds him that it really is right to celebrate. He explains his joy in the terms used earlier – dead and alive, lost and found – but this time *your brother* replaces *my son*. It is an appeal for understanding, for reconciliation, an appeal that he join them, the family, and the whole community in fellowship and festivity.

The parable responds magnificently to the initial context. The sinners are sharing the banquet. The religious leaders stand critically aloof, refusing the invitation to accept the Good News and join the party. The table fellowship of Jesus is a celebration of seeking and finding. The three parables reflect the way in which Jesus understands his ministry, what he is about. At the same time these parables reveal a great deal about Jesus' understanding of God. Jesus operates in the way he does, shares table fellowship as he does, because he knows the compassionate heart of his Father, his *all-inclusive, unconditional love, his unreserved acceptance and approval.*[6] Table fellowship expresses it all.

CONCLUSION
At the beginning of this chapter I suggested that this section of Luke's Gospel could shed much light on Salesian spirituality and mission. In recounting this parable Jesus is sharing with us his understanding of what the Father is like, and his understanding of his own mission. It is so important for Christian disciples and Salesians on mission, that our God should coincide with the God of Jesus. A God of compassion, whose love is all-inclusive and unconditional beyond our wildest dreams, whose acceptance is unreserved and freely given. We need to know this God, who comes in search of us in prodigal love. Despite his being always with him, the older brother in the parable failed to know his father. In John's Gospel Jesus makes a similar complaint of his disciples:

Have I been all this time with you and still you do not know me? (14:9)

There is a big difference between knowing about someone and really knowing them. There is a danger that aspects of the older brother's blindness, servility, joyless observance, self-righteousness have a place in our own hearts and lives.

Perhaps there are some of us who do not really know the God of Jesus. With our heads and with our lips we may acknowledge such a God, but images of other Gods frequently infringe onto our screen and distort the focus. Often such alien images can influence our prayer, the way we relate to others, our pastoral

6 P Tournier, *Guilt and Grace* (London, Hodder & Stoughton 1962), p 189.

approach and the decisions we make. Such foreign images can make it difficult for us to surrender to our God in trust. As I look back on my life I think I have struggled because of an experience I had in the sacrament of confession when on holiday at the age of eleven. As I prepared, I perused the list of sins which, according to my Salesian prayer book, Catholic boys could commit. In itself that says something. As a change from disobeying mum, or arguing with the lad next door, I thought I'd add something on the sixth commandment. After all, I'd kissed the daughter of the people we were staying with. Was that adultery? The priest behind the grille in the dark confessional box, obviously lacking in humour and imagination, tore strips off me and made me feel utterly evil and rejected by God. For several years after that, everything was sinful. From time to time that image of God recurs.

Perhaps we also need to think about the God whom we communicate to others – those with whom we live and work, and especially young people. Sometimes there is a gap between what we proclaim by our words and what we communicate indirectly through our lifestyle, our Church structures and institutions, our pastoral methods, the school curriculum, the ethos of our youth club. As officially religious people, we cannot avoid conveying an impression of our God to others. Our kindness, approachability and willingness to listen, say a great deal. Our aloofness, harshness and impatience, standing on our dignity, judgemental or critical attitudes, all communicate a certain type of God too.

Jesus' knowledge of the Father conditioned and gave life to his whole ministry. He wanted to reveal this God and make his compassion and forgiveness present in people's lives. I believe that this is what Don Bosco sought to do also. This parable of searching and finding, and its context of table fellowship, offers us rich insight into his mind and ministry. The Salesian Constitutions state: *Sent to young people by the God who is all charity, the Salesian is open and cordial, ready to make the first approach and to welcome others with unfailing kindliness, respect and patience. His love is that of a father, brother and friend, able to draw out friendship in return; this is the loving kindness so much recommended by Don Bosco.*[7]

Key words and phrases like to *seek souls, loving kindness, poor and abandoned*, which are characteristic of Don Bosco's style and mission, find their inspiration in this parable. I've often wondered how we can translate into today's

7 Constitution 15

world and culture what Jesus communicated by table fellowship in his day. It has recently dawned on me that Don Bosco achieved such a translation through what he called the *Oratory*. The Oratory was a setting in which, in the name of the God revealed by Jesus, Don Bosco welcomed the young people of his day. They were in a sense marginalised, on the fringes of religious and civil society, seriously at risk. Through the friendship, acceptance, warmth and hospitality of the Oratory, Don Bosco sought to make God present in their lives. He created a setting and an atmosphere in which they could experience God's closeness, touching and transforming their lives. He also went out searching and seeking for them in the streets and work sites of Turin, to draw them into this experience. The Oratory was a place of celebration, joy and new life.

PRAYER SUGGESTION

In prayer and reflection I suggest that we re-read chapter 15 of Luke. Imagine ourselves at Jesus' table, welcomed and accepted. Imagine ourselves also in the shoes of the younger son in the parable, and the older son. I tend to think that for most of us religious people there is more mileage in the latter. I suggest too that we spend time in the shoes of the father, and linger there. Finally, we might ask ourselves how we can translate table fellowship for today's world, and find ways of making the experience present in our different contexts.

CHAPTER THREE- COMPASSION

One of my favourite passages in the Gospel of Mark is the incident when Jesus sends out his disciples on mission.[1] The event takes place after the rejection of Jesus at Nazareth, a moment of disappointment for him. According to Mark's structuring of the ministry, the disciples have been instructed by Jesus,[2] and have been present at several of his mighty works.[3] Now they set out, charged with his authority, in order to combat evil and to call for conversion.[4] It's a kind of practical training, pastoral experience.

On their return they report to the Master all that they have taught and done. We can catch their excitement and enthusiasm, something we have probably experienced ourselves. With great sensitivity, Jesus perceives their need for a break and a rest, *many were coming and going, and they had no leisure even to eat.*[5] So Jesus invites them to come with him, by boat, to a quiet spot away from the crowds. However, the people guess their plan and thwart their attempt by reaching the intended destination before them. The text then reads:

> **As he went ashore, he saw a great crowd; and he had compassion for them, because they were like sheep without a shepherd; and he began to teach them many things.** (Mark 6:34)

Jesus realises that the people's greatest need is for instruction and enlightenment, lest they go astray in blindness and confusion. His compassion moves him to teach them *many things* or *at considerable length*. Later in the day he provides them with food by multiplying the loaves and fishes.

This passage highlights for me two aspects of Salesian spirituality: compassion and shepherding. In this chapter I would like to dwell on the theme of compassion; later I shall explore the theme of shepherding.

The Greek verb which is used to describe the reaction of Jesus to the crowds awaiting him *splanchnizesthai* means *to have compassion*. Unfortunately, it is sometimes translated differently, less accurately, and rather weakly in various

---

[1] On Mark's Gospel, see: H Anderson, *The Gospel of Mark* (London, Oliphants 1976); W Harrington, *Mark* (Dublin, Veritas 1979); M D Hooker, *The Gospel according to St Mark* (London, A&C Black 1991); D McBride, *The Gospel of Mark* (Dublin, Dominican Publications 1996); F J Moloney, *The Gospel of Mark. A Commentary* (Peabody, Hendrickson Publishers 2002); D E Nineham, *St Mark* (London, Penguin Books 1963).

[2] Mk 4:1-34   [4] Mk 6:13
[3] Mk 4:35-5:43   [5] Mk 6:31

versions of the New Testament. It is almost a technical term, and it occurs twelve times in the Gospels.

There is another Gospel incident when Jesus enquires of his disciples what people are thinking about him. And after listening to the different answers, he puts the question directly to them: *And you, who do you say that I am?* If the question were addressed to me, I would be inclined to reply by adapting the title of a book published thirty years ago by the Dutch theologian Edward Schillebeeckx, and say: *You are Christ Jesus, the sacrament of God's compassion, or the compassion of God enfleshed.* I believe that compassion is the key to understanding the revelation and identity of Jesus, and also the ministry and spirituality of Don Bosco.[6]

THE OLD TESTAMENT

The New Testament presentation of God's compassionate mercy is rooted in the Old Testament, in the experience of God which Israel had throughout her long history, and in the concepts which she used to articulate her reflection on that experience. Eloquent expression of the depth and richness of such reflection is provided in the following text from Exodus:

> **The Lord, the Lord, a God merciful and gracious, slow to anger, and abounding in steadfast love and faithfulness.** (Exodus 34:6)

Similar expressions are found in the psalms:

> **The Lord is merciful and gracious, slow to anger and abounding in steadfast love.** (Psalm 103:8)

> **But you, O Lord, are a God merciful and gracious, slow to anger and abounding in steadfast love and faithfulness.** (Psalm 86:15)

> **He has gained renown by his wonderful deeds; the Lord is gracious and merciful.** (Psalm 111:4)

Israel's insight springs from the confluence of two main streams of thought. Firstly, there is the significance which clusters around the Hebrew word *rahamim*

---

[6] See M T Winstanley, *Come and See*, p 15-22.

which expresses the attachment of one being to another. It comes from the same root as the words meaning bowels and mother's womb. So it captures shades of meaning proper to the relationship of particular love which a mother has for the child of her womb: tenderness, pity, understanding, protection, nourishing, patience, a readiness to forgive. It means to be moved to the depths of one's being.

Secondly, there is the Hebrew word *hesed* (usually rendered in Greek by *eleos*). This word implies trust and faithfulness. Used of God, it normally refers to God's faithfulness to the Covenant choice, God's pledge to Israel. God can be relied upon, can be trusted. When Israel sins, God's *hesed* takes the form of forgiveness and pardoning grace. Another dimension of the term is pity, love, sympathy evoked by distress and misfortune. This finds expression in concrete acts of deliverance, restoration, and protection.

THE NEW TESTAMENT

These two mainstreams, by which the Old Testament witnessed to its understanding of the central attribute of God, are encountered again in the New Testament presentation of the ministry of Jesus. For it was the firm conviction of the early Church that Jesus was the revelation of God's merciful compassion. As Zechariah sings in the Benedictus, in Jesus the compassionate love of God has come to visit us.[7] As well as in his teaching in Mark 6:34, the compassion of Jesus is shown in his healing a leper,[8] in his feeding the crowds,[9] in his sending disciples to minister to them,[10] in his healing the sick,[11] and giving sight to the blind,[12] and in his restoring a man to life.[13] Besides these incidents in which the technical verb is used, Jesus performs many acts of healing in response to requests for mercy. I would like to examine briefly these technical *compassion* texts, and explore their links with Salesian spirituality.

The Cleansing of the Leper

The first occasion on which the compassion of Jesus is encountered in Mark is the story of the cleansing of the leper.[14] The man's infirmity, whether it was leprosy in the technical sense, or a similar unpleasant skin disease (the NJB speaks of a *virulent* skin disease), was thought at the time to be incurable. It entailed segregation from the social and religious life of the community. A leper was obliged to wear his clothing torn and his hair dishevelled, and cry *unclean, unclean* as he moved around. He had to live apart and was forbidden to enter

7 Lk 1:78
8 Mk 1:40-45
9 Mk 8:1-3; Matt 15:32
10 Matt 9:35-38
11 Matt 14:14
12 Matt 20:29-34
13 Lk 7:11-17
14 Mk 1:40-45

any walled town or reside in a village. He was thus denied access to Jerusalem and to the Temple. This was not mainly for reasons of hygiene, but because leprosy was deemed to be evidence of, and punishment for, sin; a leper was considered unclean in the religious sense. If he entered a house, he rendered it unclean; even a chance encounter could entail ritual contamination. His life was thus a misery, a source of physical discomfort, mental anguish, and spiritual guilt. It is small wonder that lepers were dubbed *the first-born of death*, living corpses!

This outcast approaches Jesus, disregarding the regulations and apparently failing to give the customary warning. He falls to his knees at Jesus' feet, and in his isolation and hopelessness implores his help: *If only you want to, you can make me clean.*[15] The scene is charged with emotion. Jesus is *moved with compassion*; he reaches out and touches him. *Of course I want to! Be cured!* [16]

The majority of manuscripts attest to the compassion of Jesus. Other manuscripts read *moved with anger, with warm indignation*, and because this is the more difficult reading, and is omitted in the versions of Matthew and Luke, it is generally considered to be the more original. The anger of Jesus is directed against the power of evil which holds people bound. It may be a reaction to the injustice done to lepers in Israel, and to the fact that the Law and its custodians did nothing to help them.

Whatever the reading, the response of Jesus is certainly one of compassion. He bridges the dreadful chasm of separation by reaching out and touching the man. He responds to his trust, and in so doing he ignores the risk of contagion. He incurs the stigma of ritual defilement according to the Law, something no rabbi would have been prepared to do. He makes the leper whole, restores him to the life of the community, draws him into personal relationship and fellowship with himself, and enables him to experience the dawning Kingdom, the presence of a gracious God.

[15] 1:40
[16] 1:41 JB

THE SECOND FEEDING STORY IN MARK

The theme of compassion is taken up again by Mark in his description of the feeding of the four thousand. This time it is Jesus who takes the initiative, not the disciples, and his compassion is directed immediately to the alleviation of the people's physical hunger. The text reads:

> There was another occasion about this time when a huge crowd had collected, and, as they had no food, Jesus called his disciples and said to them: My heart goes out to these people; they have been with me now for three days and have nothing to eat. If I send them home hungry, they will faint on the way; some of them have a long way to go. (8:1-3)

This is a moving description of Jesus' care and concern for others in their need, a concern which leads him to reach out in a very practical way to provide for them and serve them.[17] A number of scholars hold the view that the geographical and textual context for this second multiplication, a section of stories taking place on largely Gentile territory, suggests that Mark intends to present Jesus as providing food not only for Israel, but also for the Gentiles. They too are the recipients of his compassionate outreach.

COMPASSION IN MATTHEW

The scholars say that in general Matthew tends to avoid making reference to Jesus' emotions. However, in one of his summaries, which follows a large block of miracle stories and precedes the missionary discourse, he does refer directly to Jesus' compassion.[18]

> So Jesus went round all the towns and villages teaching in their synagogues, proclaiming the good news of the Kingdom, and curing every kind of illness and infirmity. The sight of the crowds moved him to pity: they were like sheep without a shepherd, harassed and helpless. Then he said to his disciples, 'The crop is heavy, but the labourers too few; you must ask the owner to send labourers to bring in the harvest'. (Mt 9:35-38)

[17] See Matt 15:32 (for the parallel text.)

[18] On Matthew see: F W Beare, *The Gospel according to Matthew* (Oxford, Blackwell 1981); W D Davis and D C Allison, *A Critical and Exegetical Commentary on the Gospel according to Saint Matthew* (Edinburgh, T&T Clark 1988); C S Keener, *A Commentary on the Gospel of Matthew* (Grand Rapids, Eerdmans 1999); J P Meier, *Matthew* (Dublin, Veritas 1980); F J Moloney, *This is the Gospel of the Lord* (Year A) (Homebush, St Paul 1992); D Senior, *Matthew* (Nashville, Abingdon Press 1998).

The language is rather like that we met earlier in Mark.[19] The compassion of Jesus is that of a genuine shepherd deeply concerned for the welfare of his sheep, for they are in a pitiful and needy state. His response to this situation is to call the twelve and to send them out on mission, with specific instructions to cast out evil spirits and cure all kinds of sickness and disease, and to do so with his authority.[20] His compassion urges him to associate others with him in ministering to them, a ministry which in this case is mainly that of healing. It is interesting to note that in Matthew's version of the prelude to the feeding of the five thousand, the response of Jesus on coming ashore and seeing the large crowd is also one of healing, rather than teaching, as in Mark:

His heart went out to them, and he healed those who were sick. (14:14)

The final direct reference to Jesus' compassion in Matthew's Gospel is to be found in his version of the healing of the blind outside the gate of Jericho, that important and busy city some fifteen miles from Jerusalem. Mark and Luke describe the cure of one blind man; the former names him as Bartimaeus, presumably someone known to the early Christian community. Matthew, however, tells of two blind men - such duplication seems to be a stylistic trait of his. As Jesus and a large crowd are leaving the city, to follow the pilgrim way from the Jordan valley up through the hills to Jerusalem, they encounter two men by the roadside in what must have been an advantageous spot for begging. On learning that it is Jesus who is passing by, the two cry out: *'Have pity on us, Son of David.'* The crowd rebuke them and bid them keep quiet, but undeterred they plead all the more insistently for pity. Jesus stops. He has time for people in need. He calls them to him. They are only too well aware of their plight, and place all their hope in him. He asks them what they want, and, not unpredictably, they reply: *'Sir, we want our sight.'* The narrator continues:

Jesus was deeply moved, and touched their eyes. At once they recovered their sight and followed him. (Matt. 20:29-34)

Only Matthew mentions that Jesus reached out and touched the blind. Uncharacteristically, he omits the reference to their trust, or faith, contained in Mark and Luke's versions of the incident. Thus he strongly underlines the

[19] 6:34
[20] Mt 10:1

compassionate outreach of Jesus, which brings them both physical sight and the insight which spurs them on to follow him.

COMPASSION IN LUKE

Surprisingly, the sentiment of compassion is attributed explicitly to Jesus only once in Luke's Gospel, in his moving description of the raising to life of the widow's son at Nain, a small town some six miles south-east of Nazareth.[21] Jesus goes to the town accompanied by his entourage and a large crowd. As they approach the gate they meet a funeral procession moving out to the place of interment. It was the custom for burials to take place outside town, and as soon as possible after death. Our attention is focussed on the sad plight of the woman. She has lost her husband and is therefore a widow. Now her only son, the support and hope of her life, has also died.

> **When the Lord saw her, his heart went out to her, and he said: 'Do not weep.'** (7:13)

Jesus ignores the risk of incurring ritual defilement by approaching and touching the bier on which the corpse lay in a linen shroud. The bearers halt. Jesus, with a word, raises the man to life again. Showing his deep concern for the woman, he *gave him back to his mother.*

It was considered meritorious to attend funerals and share in the mourning. Consequently there were numerous witnesses to what had occurred. Their initial reaction was one of fear and awe. Then they burst into praise of God, recognising that *a great prophet has arisen among us*, and concluding, very significantly for our theme, *God has shown his care for his people*, thus echoing the words of the Benedictus.[22] The compassion of Jesus reveals the presence of God's saving mercy.

As far as I am aware, these are the Gospel incidents in which the technical term is used to describe the compassion of Jesus. The verb is also found in three parables: the parable of the Good Samaritan,[23] the parable of the Prodigal Son,[24] and the parable of the Unjust Steward.[25] When referring to the Old Testament understanding of God's compassion, I observed that God was thought to show his compassion in two ways: in forgiveness and in acts of mercy. The parables are excellent illustrations of both aspects.

[21] Lk 7:11-17
[22] 1:68
[23] Lk 10:29-37
[24] Lk 15:11-32
[25] Matt 18:23-35

CONCLUSION

Compassion is a very beautiful theme. As the Old Testament background suggests, compassion is a dynamic concept. God's compassion becomes manifest in God's reaching out to heal, support, forgive, and save his people in their need. The term compassion sums up so much about the person and ministry of Jesus. Jesus is indeed the sacrament of God's compassion. He is the sign and instrument of God's compassion, revealing it and making it present in our world. When taken together, these texts are quite powerful.

It seems to me that this theme can also provide us with insight into the person and mission of Don Bosco. It is fascinating to reflect on Don Bosco's life in the light of the Gospel episodes which we have just considered. It is almost a commentary! As Don Bosco, the young priest, wandered up and down the streets of Turin, he saw so many young people who were in need, confused, *harassed and dejected*, without work, without a place to stay, without prospects, in considerable danger, *like sheep without a shepherd*. His heart was deeply moved. That deep feeling, welling up within him, compelled him into action on their behalf. He offered these young people acceptance and friendship, provided them with a base, a hearth, a home. He removed their leprous marginalisation, alienation, and feeling of rejection by including them in his family, and giving them a sense of worth and belonging. He enabled them to experience the reality of the Kingdom of God touching their lives.

Don Bosco was concerned with their evangelisation, teaching and instructing them about Jesus and his way. He took away their inner blindness and ignorance. He offered them education, taught them trades, enabled them to develop the skills necessary to make a living. He provided them with food, sometimes in quite remarkable ways. He brought them inner healing and reconciliation, and at times physical healing too. There are stories about his raising some to life. He sought to bring them all to fuller life in so many dimensions of their being. In his concern for their welfare he sought to associate others with him in ministry. And so were born the Salesian Congregation, the Co-operator movement, and the Daughters of Mary Help of Christians. This concern extended more widely than Piedmont and Italy, as Don Bosco sent his associates to other European countries and to Latin America – the beginnings of what he saw as a worldwide outreach in the service of the young.

I think it is true to say that Don Bosco was a sacrament of the Compassion of Jesus for young people. Don Bosco's heart was fashioned after the compassionate heart of Jesus, and the fashioning of such a heart is the work of the Spirit. We have come to understand the nature and mission of the Salesian Family as: *to be in the Church, signs and bearers of the love of God for young people, especially those who are poor.[26]* It has been said that the society in which we live today in the western world is becoming increasingly lacking in compassion. There is some truth in that. The need for the Salesian charism is as urgent as ever. Yet there are so many examples of compassion in everyday life.

When my mother was dying of a form of leukaemia in a Liverpool hospital, I was deeply moved by the quality of care with which the staff surrounded her. She wasn't simply an old lady approaching her end. She was a special person, a unique individual, whose dignity was respected. As I witnessed the way in which the nursing staff treated her day after day, I understood what compassion really means.

As a young priest I suffered a period of depression, a distressing experience which, fortunately, has not recurred. I remember sitting at my desk with a selection of books open and a notepad in front of me; it was in the pre-computer days. I was going through the motions of preparing a talk, but nothing appeared on the paper. There was a knock at the door and an elderly Salesian priest came in. He stood by my side and put his arm around my shoulder as I sat there. I don't remember if he said anything, but I became aware that he knew how I was feeling, that he understood, that he believed in me and cared deeply. Whenever I think of the compassion of God, that memory springs to mind.

PRAYER SUGGESTION

Let's ponder these Gospel texts, imagining ourselves in some of the situations reflected there, and listening to the unlimited and unconditional compassion of God revealed and made present in Jesus. Let us ask the Spirit to transform our hearts, that we may more faithfully share the mission of Jesus in our world in Don Bosco's way. Perhaps we might recall experiences when we have received the gift of compassion in our time of need, or been privileged to be present in situations when compassion has been shown to others. That too is a window into God. Finally, let us examine the quality of our own compassion in the circumstances of our daily lives.

[26] Constitution 2.

CHAPTER FOUR – THE GOOD SHEPHERD

In the last twenty years or so there has been in the Salesian Family a rediscovery of the image of the Shepherd as a symbol of the person and work of Jesus, and as an example for ministry. The Salesian Constitutions maintain that the Christ of the Gospel is the source of the Salesian spirit, and observe that as we read the Gospel *we become more aware of certain aspects of the figure of the Lord.* Amongst these various aspects is included *the preoccupation of the Good Shepherd who wins hearts by gentleness and self-giving.*[1] The motif was chosen for the cross which was minted to celebrate the centenary of Don Bosco's death in 1988. In this chapter I would like to share some reflections with you on this shepherd theme as it is presented in the Old and New Testaments, in the hope that we may deepen our understanding of our spirituality, and be drawn to live it more fully.

We are centuries away from the time of Jesus. The culture gap is enormous. Most of the places where we live and work are in towns and cities. In the retreat centre which is my home, however, we are surrounded by sheep. The land is rented out to a sheep farmer. Although he uses a tractor and Land Rover and a couple of beautiful dogs, he cares for his sheep with remarkable devotion. This is particularly the case at lambing time, when he comes at all hours of the day and night to assist the ewes, and in the depth of winter when there is snow, and food has to be provided. The dreadful outbreak of foot and mouth disease, and the images of the culling of thousands of sheep, increased the awareness of the nation to this aspect of our agrarian economy and the country way of life. It was a heartbreaking time for the farmers. For my summer holidays I tend to go walking on the fells of the Lake District. Last summer the absence of sheep was quite eerie. So the biblical imagery, I believe, can still speak to us today.[2]

THE OLD TESTAMENT

To begin, I recall the scene from Mark's Gospel on which we reflected in the previous chapter, when Jesus attempts to take the disciples by boat to a quiet spot away from the crowds, and on arriving finds the people already there.

---

[1] Constitution 11
[2] This chapter is a revision of a chapter I wrote in *Into Your Hands* (Homebush, St Pauls 1994), p 69-88. I am grateful for permission to make use of this material.

> **When he came ashore and saw a large crowd, his heart went out to them, because they were like sheep without a shepherd.** (6:34)

We found similar wording in Matthew:

> **The sight of the crowds moved him to pity: they were like sheep without a shepherd, harassed and helpless.** (Mt 9:36)

In both these passages there is a link between compassion and shepherding, twin elements at the heart of Salesian spirituality.

The description of the people in these texts as *sheep without a shepherd* is found in several Old Testament locations. For instance, Moses pleads with God to appoint a leader for the community, *who shall go out before them and come in before them, who shall lead them out and bring them in, so that the congregation of the Lord may not be like sheep without a shepherd.3* As a result, Joshua is anointed and invested with authority. The prophet Micaiah,4 when consulted by King Ahab concerning the wisdom of proceeding to attack Ramoth-gilead, is pressurised into disclosing his vision of the army in disarray: *I saw all Israel scattered on the mountains, like sheep that have no shepherd; and the Lord said, 'These have no master; let each one go home in peace.'5* Matthew refers to Jesus as having been sent to the lost sheep of the House of Israel,6 and he describes Jesus as directing the disciples specifically to them when they go out on their initial mission. In his infancy narrative, in which many of the important themes of the Gospel receive a first airing, Matthew presents the role of Jesus, who was born in the city of the shepherd-king David, *as a ruler who is to shepherd my people Israel.7*

The people of Israel were initially nomadic, and a strongly pastoral orientation continued after life became more settled. In Jesus' day there was still much sheep and goat farming. It is only to be expected, therefore, that the images of shepherd and flock should feature prominently in their literature.

In reading this literature we find that God is held to be the Shepherd of Israel, though explicit references are rare. In blessing Joseph and his sons, Jacob

32

3 Num 27:17 NJB
4 1 Kings 22:17
5 cf also Zech 10:2
6 15:27
7 2:6, citing Mic 5:1

s

(

l

tors Abraham and Isaac walked, the
to this day,[8] and recalls that Joseph
:pherd, the Rock of Israel.[9] There are
.ord is my shepherd,[10] and Hear us,
ock .[11]

itly referred to as sheep or flock: Then
uided them in the wilderness like a
he shepherd role of God is strongly

;reen pastures; he leads
23:2)[13]

of God's relationship with Israel find

shepherd; he will gather
carry them in his bosom,
and gently .....   :r sheep. (Is 40:11)

The returning exiles are described as sheep coming home to the evening fold.[14]

Frequently in the Old Testament, God is thought of as delegating this shepherd-role to others. Some leaders, such as Moses, Joshua and David, fulfil their task well. But it often occurs that those to whom the flock has been entrusted prove unfaithful, and fulfil their responsibilities inadequately. This leads to situations in which the sheep are described as *harassed and dejected*. The wicked shepherds of Israel are trenchantly and vehemently upbraided by the prophets, notably Jeremiah and Ezekiel:

**Woe to the shepherds who destroy and scatter the
sheep of my pasture! says the Lord.** (Jer 23:1)

These shepherds have fed themselves rather than their sheep, have failed to strengthen the weak, have not healed the sick nor bound up the crippled. They have not sought the lost, nor brought back the strayed; they have ruled with force and harshness.[15] As a result of such blatant lack of care the sheep stray far and wide, a prey to wild animals.

---

[8] Gen 48:15
[9] Gen 49:24
[10] Ps 23:1
[11] Ps 80:1
[12] Ps 78:52 ; cf Ps 71:4; 79:13; 95:7; 100:3; Hos 4:16
[13] cf Ps 28:9; 68:7; 77:20; 121:4
[14] Is 49:9-10
[15] Ezek 34:4; cf Jer 2:8; 10:21; 12:10

It is clear what a real shepherd is expected to be, and to do. So God pledges that he will himself go to their rescue, and seek out the lost, bind up the crippled, strengthen the weak, watch over the fat and strong, bring the strays back, and provide excellent pasture.[16] The Lord then goes on to promise that he will give them shepherds after his own heart who will care for them, feed them with knowledge and understanding, and remove their fear and dismay.[17] Finally, God says:

> **I will set up over them one shepherd, my servant**
> **David, and he shall feed them: he shall feed them**
> **and be their shepherd.** (Ezek 34:23)[18]

Jesus is considered as fulfilling these prophetic expectations for he responds to the needs of the *harassed and helpless* crowds, by teaching, healing, feeding and sending others to minister to them. He is the awaited messianic Shepherd. The Fourth Evangelist takes up this insight and develops it with considerable originality and depth.[19]

THE FOURTH GOSPEL
THE SHEPHERD IN JOHN 10

I think it is useful to remind ourselves of the context in which John presents the parable and explanations of the Good Shepherd. The theme is found at the end of the Evangelist's lengthy treatment of the feast of Tabernacles, a period in which the hostility to Jesus grows significantly. The Shepherd theme is closely integrated with the preceding incident, the magnificently constructed narrative of the man born blind, in which Jesus is presented as the light of the world.[20] Towards the end of that episode is posed the question of the genuine leadership of Israel. The religious authorities, so full of their own importance, so self-assured were trapped in their legalistic parameters. They have scorned the man and thrown him out of the synagogue, instead of welcoming him and rejoicing in his good fortune. By contrast, Jesus has gone in search of him and led him to the insight of faith. The incident concludes with a confrontation and irrevocable division between Jesus, the light, and these Pharisees, who, hardened in their blindness and sin, have forfeited the right to lead the people.[21] There is no reference to a change in audience, no break in the narrative as we move into the shepherding imagery.

34

[16] Ezek 34:11-16   [17] Jer 3:15; 23:4   [18] cf 34:30-31;37:24   [20] 9:1-41   [21] 9:39-41
[19] In my treatment of material from the Fourth Gospel I am particularly indebted to: C K Barrett, *The Gospel according to John* (London, SPC 1978); T L Brodie, *The Gospel according to John* (Oxford, OUP 1993); R E Brown, *The Gospel according to John* (London, Chapmans 1972), vols; R A Culpepper, *Anatomy of the Fourth Gospel* (Philadelphia, Fortress 1983); C H Dodd, *The Interpretation of the Fourth Gospel* (Cambridge, CUP 1968); B Lindars, *The Gospel of John* (London, Oliphants 1972); F J Moloney, *The Gospel of John* (Collegeville, The Liturgic Press 1998); R Schnackenburg, *The Gospel of John* (London, B&O vol 1 1968, vol 2 1980, vol 3 1982); M W G Stibbe, John. Readings (Sheffiel JSOT Press 1993). See also J Beutler and R T Fortna (eds), *The Shepherd Discourse of John 10 and its Context* (Cambridge, CUP 1991).

The imagery is continued into the following feast, that of Dedication, during which there are attempts to stone Jesus[22] and later to arrest him.[23] Jesus is forced to withdraw. Subsequently, despite the disciples' protestations, he takes the risk of returning to Judea in order to raise Lazarus. The result of this sign is that the priests and Pharisees call a meeting which is, in effect, the Johannine equivalent of the trial of Jesus. There the decision is taken that Jesus should die. In the course of chapter ten there are many allusions to what is to follow. It is against this background of confrontation and under the shadow of this threat, rather than an idyllic pastoral setting, that the theme of the Shepherd is developed.

Figurative Discourse and the Reaction: 10:1-6

The setting is a sheepfold in the early morning. This could consist of a square formed by stone walls on a hillside, or, as seems more likely here, a courtyard in front of a house protected by a surrounding wall. It was not uncommon for several small flocks to be jointly penned at night, and often someone would be hired to watch them. The fundamental issue, which ties in with the previous incident, is that of the legitimate and illegitimate shepherds of the people. Two contrasts are drawn. Firstly, the man who attempts to gain access to the fold by scaling the wall is contrasted with the one who enters by the gate. The former is classed as a thief and a robber. The true shepherd, to whom the sheep belong, is openly admitted by the gatekeeper.

The second area of contrast focuses on the different relationship which the shepherd and the stranger have to the sheep. On entering the fold the shepherd calls by name the sheep which he owns. It is not unusual for Palestinian shepherds to have nicknames for at least some of their sheep. Here the implication is that the shepherd has an affectionate name for each of them. They, for their part, recognise his voice and respond, and he assists their awkward exit. Once in the open, the shepherd strides out ahead, and the sheep fall in behind and follow.[24] The stranger, on the other hand, has no relationship with the sheep, so they do not recognise his voice, and refuse to follow him.

Those listening to Jesus fail to understand his figurative language, so Jesus offers some clarification, concentrating firstly on the image of the gate,[25] and then that of the shepherd.[26] His explanation creates further division amongst his audience.[27]

---

[22] 10:31
[23] 10:39
[24] Num 27:17; Ps 77:52; Ezek 34:13
[25] 10:7-10
[26] 10:11-18
[27] 10:19-21

Twofold Explanation and Response: 10:7-21

In verses 7-10 Jesus takes up the image of the gate or door of the sheepfold, and claims that he alone is the gate. Others, be they messianic pretenders, priestly politicians or religious leaders, he classes as thieves and robbers. Their approaches are illegitimate. There is only one door, one way, one source of revelation and salvation. The shepherding of Jesus is unique and exclusive.

The sheep who gain access to the fold through him find safety and security; they have the freedom to come and go at will, and are assured of pasture.[28] It is through Jesus, and through him alone, that the sheep have access to the messianic community, and enjoy real freedom and eschatological salvation, with its countless blessings.[29] Once more, with a further polemic thrust, Jesus contrasts himself with the thief in the first verse, whose aim is to kill the sheep, and as Satanic agent wreak ruin,[30] whereas the purpose for which Jesus has come is to offer the sheep rich, abundant and lasting life, life in all its fullness, the life *from above*, the life of God.[31]

In the second part of his explanation, the point of identification switches from gate to shepherd, and the emphasis rests firmly on the quality of his care for the flock. His *goodness* and dedication lead him to lay down his life on their behalf, which far surpasses anything suggested in the Old Testament treatment of this motif. A shepherd's life did entail risk, as is illustrated in the story of David.[32] The joy amongst the shepherd's friends and neighbours in the parable of the lost sheep[33] is probably caused in part by his safe return.

The good shepherd's generosity stands in stark contrast with the behaviour of the hireling. As soon as danger looms in the form of a predatory wolf, he takes to his heels and abandons the flock, which suffers harassment and is scattered. The shepherd's care stems from the fact that the sheep belong to him, whereas the hireling is concerned with his pocket and his skin, and has no personal interest in the sheep. Another differentiating factor is the mutual knowledge which exists between the sheep and himself: *I know my own sheep and my sheep know me*. Such knowledge is not of the theoretical, intellectual type; as also in the Old Testament, it denotes intimacy, relationship, friendship-bonding. Once again the Evangelist bursts out of the original framework of the parables, asserting that this relationship is patterned on and results from the relationship between the Father and Jesus. The implications of this statement are spelled out

36

[28] Ps 118:20
[29] Ps 23:2; Is 49:9; Ezek 34:12-15
[30] Jn 8:44
[31] cf 3:16-17
[32] 1 Samuel 17:34

[33] Lk 15:4-7

more fully in the discourses at the Supper.

A new dimension is introduced when Jesus refers to other sheep of his, which do not belong to the fold of Israel. These will listen to his voice; it is his task to lead them too. A new flock, comprising both Jew and Greek, will then come into existence under the one shepherd. This will be brought about only as a result of his death and exaltation, for he *would die for the nation, and not for the nation alone, but to gather together the scattered children of God.*34 It is in the context of the Father's love, that love whereby God gave the son,35 that Jesus will freely fulfil the mandate which he has received, that he should lay down his life and take it up again. It is then that the fullness of life will become available and the new community will be created. Here again, we glimpse the depth of the Shepherd's relationship with the Father, and his total orientation to the fulfilment of his mission, the Father's saving plan.

DIALOGUE AT THE FEAST OF DEDICATION: 10:22-39

There is now a change of season. Several months later Jesus is again, or still, in Jerusalem, walking in the temple precincts in the Portico of Solomon, which afforded protection from the cold easterly wind. It is the feast of Dedication, which commemorated the rededication of the Temple by Judas Maccabaeus after its desecration by the Syrians.36 In the course of this carefully structured section, which erupts into violence, Jesus takes up the imagery of shepherd and sheep again. The fact that his opponents do not believe what he has said, do not listen to his voice, nor accept the credentials of his works, indicates clearly that they are not sheep of his flock. The earlier explanations of the original parabolic speech concentrated on the gate and the shepherd; now the emphasis rests on the sheep. The sheep that belong to him do listen to his voice; they are known by him and they follow him. They receive from him the gift of eternal life and so will not perish. Their safety is secured, for they cannot be snatched from his care, protected as they are by one who is no hireling. Jesus adds that really it is the Father who has given him the sheep; the Father is the ultimate source of their safety and security. He concludes with that astounding climactic statement: *My Father and I are one.*37

This assertion is, in this context, a statement of the Evangelist's conviction that not only is Jesus the fulfilment of the promises and hopes concerning the messianic shepherd, but far more, namely that the shepherding of God and that

34 11:52
35 3:16
36 cf 1 Macc 1:54; 4:41-61; 2 Macc 6:1f
37 10:30

of Jesus are one. In Jesus the compassionate and solicitous love of God is enfleshed, is savingly present, offering life and communion.

THE SHEPHERD IN JOHN 21

The theme of the shepherd is found also in the scene in the garden where Jesus allows himself to be arrested, making provision for the safe departure of his disciples,[38] and also in the encounter between the Risen One and Magdalen.[39] But it is the encounter between the Risen Jesus and Simon Peter by the Sea of Tiberias which takes our theme further.[40]

After a fruitless night's fishing, the stranger on the shore suggests that Peter and his companions try again on the starboard side. They obey and make a fine catch. After dragging the net to shore they find that Jesus has prepared for them a breakfast of bread and fish on a charcoal fire, a reminder of the charcoal fire in the courtyard of the denials. Attention is then focused on Jesus and Peter.

Jesus addresses Peter as *Simon, son of John* as at their original encounter, after Andrew had introduced them, when Jesus changed his name to Cephas, the Rock.[41] Three times he asks Peter whether he loves him, and three times the chastened Peter replies: *Yes, Lord, you know I love you*. Rather than boast as before, he simply entrusts himself to Jesus who knows his heart. Each time Jesus responds to Peter by telling him to feed his flock.

We are meant to understand this episode firstly as Peter's rehabilitation. The threefold questioning and avowal of love are linked with the threefold denial. Jesus, the shepherd reaching out to his wayward sheep, is affording Peter the opportunity of making up in some way for having let him down so badly. He assures him of his generous forgiveness, measured by the awesome responsibility he subsequently bestows.

Secondly, the scene depicts Peter's pastoral commissioning. Some maintain that the threefold repetition of the command to tend the lambs and sheep adds to the obvious solemnity of the occasion. It is significant that Jesus insists on love as a necessary prerequisite for this role, love for him in the first place. Peter must be utterly devoted to his Master; only then can he be entrusted with the care of the flock. Mission flows from relationship. The flock remains the flock of Jesus; the sheep continue to belong to Jesus - *my sheep*. They are handed into

[38] 18:1-11
[39] 20:14-16
[40] 21:15-19
[41] 1:41-42

Peter's safe keeping. Just as God, in the Old Testament, delegated his shepherd role to others, so does Jesus in the New.

In the biblical tradition the role of shepherd implies authority.[42] Peter shares in the authority of Jesus. However, in delineating the characteristic traits of the Good Shepherd, John omits all reference to power, status, superiority, prerogatives. He emphasises aspects of pastoral care: knowledge and familiarity, affectionate solicitude and help, protection, and dedication.

The outstanding note of John's portrayal of the Good Shepherd is self-giving, self-sacrifice. Our current text moves naturally to the same theme, as Jesus indicates that Peter will also share his destiny of violent death. During the dialogue at the supper, Peter boasted that he was ready to lay down his life for Jesus;[43] subsequent events proved him mistaken. Now the Risen Lord assures him that he will express his avowed love precisely in this way:[44]

> **...but when you are old you will stretch out your arms, and a stranger will bind you fast, and carry you where you have no wish to go.** (21:18)

Scholars dispute whether these words imply crucifixion specifically, or simply captivity as a prelude to death. For the Evangelist they clearly indicate that Peter will follow the shepherd pattern of Jesus and glorify God by obediently surrendering to death.

Finally, Jesus adds the injunction *Follow me*. At the supper, when Peter asked where he was going, Jesus answered:

> **I am going where you cannot follow me now, but one day you will.** (13:36)

Now he can follow him, because he is no longer self-confident and is empowered from above. He can take the way of genuine discipleship which always calls for self-giving, and which in his case will demand martyrdom.

---

[42] 1 Chron 19:6; 2 Sam 5:2
[43] 13:36
[44] 15:13

CONCLUSION

The scriptural image of the shepherd is certainly a window into the mystery of God and God's dealings with us. It illustrates God's provident care and healing love. It is also a symbol which captures so expressively the reality and role of Jesus. It captures his compassion, his teaching and revealing, his healing and solicitude, the life-giving and liberating intimacy of his relating, his faithful protecting, and his commitment to us to the extent of dying for us. It is an image which beckons us to reflection and contemplation, and to a response of trusting love.

This image also serves as an example for Salesian life and ministry. It is a key to what we mean by the Preventive System. Salesians are called to teach and evangelise, to lead to enriched understanding; to heal and strengthen the weak, bind up the broken and crippled, feed and nourish, foster growth and fuller life. We are to know our sheep by name, guide them with gentleness, love them with compassion and deep affection. We are to create a space for freedom, a climate of trust, removing fear and dismay. We are to be prepared to search for and find the lost, and experience the joy and burden of restoration. We are to protect the sheep, being prepared to risk, to suffer, even to die. We are to shun harshness, tyranny, exploitation, self-interest, and avoid all forms of force and neglect. *Shepherd* is indeed a symbol explosive with challenge.

As we reflect on the model Shepherd and the background of this image, we are obliged to acknowledge the cost of such love in our daily life and ministry. It is also necessary to accept the probability of conflict, struggle and pain. Contrary to the indications of some forms of religious art, the shepherd image is far from romantic or comfortable. It is always overshadowed by the cross. The invitation to feed the sheep, to be a source of life for us, draws us to live in that shadow.

The shepherd imagery calls us individually and collectively to examine and evaluate the quality of our living, caring, and ministering. We may find that changes are required, changes in structures and pastoral strategy, changes of attitude and style. Such practical changes, however, will be unfruitful if they do not stem from a change of heart. The Fourth Evangelist indicates this by having Jesus preface his pastoral commissioning with the question: *Do you love me?* Mission and ministry flow from relationship, action from contemplation. We need to allow the Spirit to transform our hearts, fashioning and shaping them after the pattern of Jesus' shepherd heart. Our dispositions, values, outlook, will then become more like his. As we grow to know more intimately his shepherding love for us and for all the sheep, we will be moved, motivated and empowered to continue his mission. We need to do so according to his style, feeding the sheep in a manner which is a more faithful replica of his. We shall then become signs and bearers of God's shepherding love to all whose lives we touch.

PRAYER SUGGESTION

Pick a few of the phrases which describe God's shepherding, listen to them being spoken to you, and see how this resonates within. Examine the list of shepherding qualities, and see how much this describes your way of dealing with those in your care. How do you feel about the cost of shepherding?

CHAPTER FIVE – VINE AND BRANCHES

One of the most beautiful sights in many parts of the world is a vineyard in the early morning sun, as it catches the light and hugs the hillside. The same was true of the Palestine of Jesus. It is only to be expected that, as well as enjoying the fruit of the vine, Jesus, who was so in touch with his environment, should have used this imagery in his teaching. In this he was following a familiar and fertile tradition in the religious history of his people. References to vineyards and vines punctuate the Old Testament, and are frequent in the Synoptic parables,[1] but it is the use of this imagery in John which I propose to choose as the topic for our consideration in this chapter. It is another area of scripture which underpins Salesian spirituality.[2]

CONTEXT

The Fourth Evangelist presents the metaphor of vine and branches within the context of the Lord's Supper, where he draws together in a sublime synthesis comprising three or four separate discourses the message of Jesus for *his own*. This section of the Gospel, consisting of chapters 13-17, has a lengthy and complex history. The repetitive nature of the text can be disconcerting, and suggests the eventual sewing together of several forms of the tradition, continually reworked over many years, as the community recalled and retold the story of Jesus.

These discourses contain some of John's loftiest and most perceptive reflections on the person and role and mystery of the Son. They also provide some of his warmest and most moving insights into Jesus' humanity. Taking these five chapters in one wide sweep, I find so much that is breathtaking and poignant. Jesus, aware of his impending return to the Father through the suffering of his *hour*, shares his deepest thoughts and feelings with those with whom he has been sharing his everyday life. It is fascinating to observe the subtle shift of mood and tone. We catch the pain of parting and separation, the devastation of betrayal by a friend, a protective concern for the future well-being of his disciples, an ache and longing to remain with them, a strong desire to reassure, and, above all, the amazing richness of his affection. From this enormous wealth

[1] cf Mk 12:1-9; Mt 20:1-6; 21:28-32; 21:33-41; Lk 13:6-9; 20:9-16
[2] This chapter is a revised version of a chapter in *Into Your Hands*. I am grateful for permission to use this material.

of material I would like to reflect on three points: disclosure, friendship and fruitfulness.

A WAY OF DISCIPLESHIP
DISCLOSURE
At one point in the section where he uses the imagery of the vine and branches Jesus says:

> **I have disclosed to you everything that I heard from my Father.** (15:15 NJB)

Throughout this Gospel Jesus is presented as the Revealer. He is the Word of God, the supreme communication and unique self-disclosure of God, enfleshed.

> **No one has ever seen God; God's only Son, he who is nearest to the Father's heart, has made him known.** (1:18 NJB)

> **Not that anyone has seen the Father except the one who is from God; he has seen the Father.** (6:46)

Much of John's rich imagery suggests this revelation motif. Jesus is the light of the world,[3] a theme illustrated in the cleverly constructed drama of the cure of the man born blind. He is the source of living water, a claim developed in the early part of his encounter with the Samaritan woman,[4] and thought to refer primarily to the revelation he brings. He is the bread of life, which in the first part of the famous discourse of chapter six is generally considered to be a symbol for revelation and teaching.

Jesus knows the heart of God, the mind of God. He states that he has been taught by the Father;[5] the Father dwelling in him is the source of the words he speaks.[6] His mission is to make the Father known, and at the conclusion of his final prayer, he can claim to have revealed to *his own* the Father's *name*, the very being of God.[7] This he does by his teaching, his words, and by his actions, the signs which he works; but he does so especially by who he is, and such disclosure is much more immediate.

> **If you know me, you will know my Father also... Whoever has seen me has seen the Father.** (14:7-9)

3 9:5
4 4:1-42
5 8:28
6 14:10
7 17:26

There is no need for special visions or theophanies,[8] for, in disclosing himself to his disciples, Jesus is the window into the mystery of God.

FRIENDSHIP

Such self-disclosure is an expression of Jesus' love, as he affirms:

> **those who love me will be loved by my Father, and I will love them and reveal myself to them.** (14:21)

It is also an invitation to intimacy, to friendship, to the one-ing and bonding of persons, to a shared existence like vine and branches.

> **I made your name known to them, and I will make it known, so that the love with which you have loved me may be in them, and I in them.** (17:26)

The theme of *being in, remaining in, abiding, indwelling*, is a key Johannine concept, and connotes being immersed in love, surrounded by love, with an assurance of permanence. It is the central idea of the first section of the vine allegory.[9] Jesus is the true vine, and issues to the disciples the invitation:

> **Dwell in me, as I in you** (15:4a NJB)

- or, as another translation puts it,

> **Make your home in me as I make mine in you. As the Father has loved me, so I have loved you; abide in my love.** (15:9)

This love theme is taken up again in the next section:[10]

> **You are my friends if you do what I command you. I do not call you servants any longer, because the servant does not know what the master is doing; but I have called you friends, because I have made known to you everything that I have heard from my Father.** (15:14-15)

44

[8] cf Exod 33:18
[9] 15:1-11
[10] 15:12-17

I call you fri   rwhelmingly rich, for it is
rooted in th(Father. It is a love *to the*
uttermost,[11]   )ne for one's friends than
to give one':   'he *supreme gift, and the*
mark of lov(m self-disclosure, which
distinguishe

The friendsh   f concern and solicitude,
and the firm

                                        anish your

                                        There are
                                        ouse; if it
                                        am going
                                        f I go and
                                        n and take
                                        y be also...

Father, I do not pray you to take them out of the
world, but to keep them from the evil one...Father,
they are your gift to me; and my desire is that they
may be with me where I am. (17:15 & 24)

Jesus' words of love flow out, wave after wave, drawing us into the sea of his intimacy.

FRUITFULNESS

In the context of the imagery of the vine and branches, this intimacy, friendship, this *abiding*, this mutuality, is intrinsically linked with fruitfulness. The vinedresser cuts away the fruitless or dead branch, and prunes the fruitful branch to make it bear even more.[15]

No branch can bear fruit by itself, but only if it
remains united with the vine; no more can you bear
fruit, unless you remain united with me. (15:4)

[11] 13:1
[12] 15:13; cf 10:18
[13] C K Barrett, *The Gospel according to St John* (London, SPCK 1978), p.477
[14] 16:27
[15] 15:2

> **Anyone who dwells in me, as I dwell in him, bears much fruit; apart from me you can do nothing.** (15:5)

> **This is how my Father is glorified: you are to bear fruit in plenty and so be my disciples.** (15:8)

The total dependency of branch on vine could not be more forcefully stated. Everything hinges on the disciple's incorporation in Jesus. Life and empowerment are drawn from the vine.

I think that the Evangelist sees fruitfulness at three levels.

Firstly, the love which Jesus has for us is a love which leads to our personal growth and development - to our having life in all its fullness. Our mutual *abiding* leads to deeper love, as love responds to love, and we are caught up in the meaning of his life and being, his loving surrender to the Father's will. *Abiding* includes the element of ongoing commitment. This love finds its natural expression in obedience, according to the pattern of Jesus' loving surrender to the Father's will.

Secondly, our response to his loving us leads to a reaching out to share life and love with others. Jesus' commandment is that we love one another, and the pattern and model of such servant loving is his own love for us.[16] It is a love prepared to wash feet and to give self in death. The focus of such loving seems to be the Christian community.

Thirdly, there is a wider missionary outreach, as Jesus, in language which has a more formal and official ring, tells his disciples:

> **You did not choose me but I chose you. And I appointed you to go and bear fruit, fruit that will last.** (15:16)

The commissioning takes place later in the narrative when the Risen Jesus appears to the disciples in the upper room, and breathes the Spirit into them, saying:

> **As the father sent me, so I send you.** (20:21)

[16] 15:12; 13:15; 13:34-35

Mission flows from mutuality. The fruitfulness of mission springs from the quality of our love for Jesus which flows out in self-giving service to others.

Jesus' statement about his choosing us, highlights the giftedness of his disclosure, of his friendship, and of our ensuing fruitfulness and sharing of mission. God has gratuitously taken the initiative in sending the Son as the light of the world, as the self-disclosure of God, and as the source of *eternal life*, the communicator of the life and love of God. The Son has freely chosen the disciples to be recipients of this revelation and sharers in this life. He has drawn them into an *abiding* relationship of love, into a community of love, and into the sharing of his mission. As disciples, our love for others bears witness to our relationship with Jesus. It reflects Jesus' love for us, and the mutual love which exists eternally between the Father and the Son. If we remain in the vine, our love continues to be revelation and source of life for others.

In the triadic pattern of disclosure-friendship-fruitfulness, John offers us a paradigm of Christian existence, Christian aliveness, this dynamic gift of our *abiding* in Christ Jesus. The elements ebb and flow in an ongoing movement of life and growth; they overlap in the cyclic interplay between contemplation and action. This pattern can, I believe, also shed some light on our relationships and mission, and it also offers an interesting perspective from which to view Don Bosco.

A MODEL FOR RELATIONSHIPS

One of our fundamental human drives and needs moves us in the direction of relating to others, to *connectedness*, and, more deeply, in the direction of friendship, interpersonal intimacy. That this is so comes as no surprise if we are indeed fashioned in God's image, and if, to use St Aelred of Rievaulx' rendering of 1 John 4:16, *God is friendship, and those who dwell in friendship are dwelling in God, and God in them.*

To reach human and Christian fulfilment we need to be able to establish and sustain real friendships. We are made for and called to friendship. It was St Thomas Aquinas who wrote that the highest form of love is friendship. Friendship is the most beautiful of all human experiences. It can break us open so that we can know God. One of the most penetrating descriptions of friendship is, I believe, that contained in the passage which we have been considering:

Dwell in me as I dwell in you or *Make your home in me as I make mine in you*, a union of mind and heart and being, in which unique individuality and profound interrelatedness coalesce and enhance each other.

An integral part of the development of human relationships and friendship and mutuality is self-disclosure. This is an ongoing process, *whereby we freely share information about ourselves in a personal way.* We can, it is true, get to know quite a lot about a person through observation, sensitive listening, and intuition. But here I am referring to the unfolding of our story *from the inside*, the revealing of aspects of ourselves and our experience, our mystery, which are normally hidden, often very private, always sacred.

Such disclosure presupposes a certain level of self-awareness; a lack of such awareness is one of the main barriers to communication. Disclosure consists in a sharing of ideas, aspirations, hopes and dreams, or anxieties, fears, struggles and problems; a confiding of feelings and experiences, our disappointments perhaps and disillusionment, our failures and brokenness, our joys and vision and faith. It demands a willingness to trust, to entrust oneself to the other; a willingness to become vulnerable, to dismantle some of our defences, to acknowledge in the hearing of another what is inside. One of the deepest needs of the human heart is to be understood, accepted and loved. *We will only be known and loved as we really are, insofar as we are willing to reveal our true selves to others. We can only do this to the extent that we are in touch with the deeper things in our hearts.*[17]

If such disclosure is received, with what Henri Nouwen calls *hospitality*, and Evelyn Woodward *empathy*, with attention and non-judgemental acceptance, appreciation, warmth and understanding, the relationship tends to grow.[18] Often reciprocal disclosure is called forth, at least later; friendship and interpersonal intimacy develop. On the other hand, criticism, moralising or rejection when one has been prepared to share, can be devastatingly hurtful and destructive. Such responses reinforce mistrust, low self-esteem, fear and defensiveness, which are the greatest obstacles to disclosure and growth, and which lock relationships in cramping ordinariness and superficiality.

Genuine friendships are fruitful and life-giving. The acceptance and affirmation of another enable self-acceptance. It gives a sense of worth, a sense of being at

[17] P Collins, *Intimacy and the Hungers of the Heart* (Dublin, Columba 1991), p 111.
[18] See H Nouwen, *Reaching Out* (London, Collins 1976), p 61-101; E Woodward, *Poets, Prophets and Pragmatists* (Melbourne, Collins Dove 1987), p 55.

home and at peace with oneself, the realisation that *it is good to be me*, a feeling of well-being. I become more self-aware and more integrated. Awareness that I am known, understood, accepted and loved is liberating. It bestows confidence and assurance, and releases creativity. Where friendship is lacking we find apathy, flatness, deadness, boredom, isolation, cynicism. Friendship brings meaning and aliveness, zest and purposefulness. It actualises so much potential, latent within. Gifts and capabilities blossom. Qualities of kindness and compassion and generosity grow, as we are freed and empowered to reach out and genuinely serve others. Our lives become so much more fruitful and life-giving. For love, of its nature, spills out and soaks all around, like mountain water bursting over the edge of a wayside trough.

It is encouraging, I feel, to find in the Salesian Constitutions statements like the following: *In an atmosphere of brotherly friendship we share our joys and sorrows, and we are partners in our apostolic plans and experiences.[19] Consecrated chastity....develops in us a Christian sense of personal relationships, encourages true friendships, and helps to make the community a family.[20] To live and work together is for us Salesians a fundamental requirement and a sure way of fulfilling our vocation. This is why we come together in communities, where our love for each other leads us to share all we have in a family spirit, and so create communion between person and person. The community is a reflection of the mystery of the Trinity: there we find a response to the deep aspirations of the heart, and we become for the young signs of love and unity.[21]*

CONCLUSION

I believe that these three headings: disclosure, friendship and fruitfulness, offer us an interesting perspective by which we can view Don Bosco. Don Bosco disclosed so much. With his Salesians and young people, he shared his dreams and ideals, his values and feelings, his pain, his joy, his love. He disclosed to them also all he had been taught by the Father, his knowledge and experience of God's presence and saving design. Such disclosure led others to make his ideals their own. His disclosure was certainly an invitation to friendship, an invitation so magnetic that few could resist; an invitation so personal that everyone was convinced that he was Don Bosco's favourite. Such friendship naturally led them to make their own the values which they saw in him. He was the *friend of youth*. Friendship was at the heart of his educational and

[19] Constitution 51
[20] Constitution 83
[21] Constitution 49.

evangelising style. Young people had to know that they were genuinely loved. Many were drawn to share his way of life and his mission. His warm love was immensely fruitful. Wolves turned into lambs, gang-leaders to apostles. There were oratories and schools, parishes and hostels, a new religious family, a vibrant spirituality, a mission reaching ever more widely towards the youth of the world. And it all continues today.

I am deeply convinced that the words of Jesus in John 15 draw us into the heart of Jesus, and tell us a great deal about the heart of Don Bosco. They therefore take us right to the heart of Salesian spirituality, whilst providing us with a pattern to guide our living.

PRAYER SUGGESTION

We can imagine Jesus addressing us with words and phrases from John 15. Repeat them over and over again, allowing them to sink into our being. We can examine the quality of our disclosure, and the obstacles to openness which we find in ourselves. We can reflect on our experience of friendship, and what it means to us and demands of us.

CHAPTER SIX - HOLY GROUND

In this chapter I would like to examine the basis for two interrelated aspects of Salesian spirituality: the value of what is ordinary in daily life, and joyful optimism. Initial inspiration is derived from a fascinating extract from the Old Testament, the story of Moses and the Burning Bush.

OLD TESTAMENT

This passage follows the basic pattern of a biblical vocation narrative. Moses is involved in his ordinary daily work, minding his father-in-law's sheep. The angel of the Lord suddenly and unexpectedly interrupts him. He is addressed by name, for there is always something original and deeply personal about such an encounter. Without hesitation Moses responds positively: *Here I am*. Later he is given the mission to lead his people to freedom from their Egyptian slavery.

The aspect which I find particularly interesting is the feature special to this narrative, when Moses is told to come no closer. He is to remove his sandals from his feet, because the place on which he is standing is Holy Ground. God's approach to Moses is an invitation to closeness, and at the same time to reverence and wonder.

Moses was called to friendship with God, invited to walk with God, to be closely involved in the sequence of events that form part of the foundation myth of Israel. His relationship with God was, I believe, quite unique in the whole of the Old Testament. He is *the* prophet, par excellence. Through him the people were not only liberated from slavery, but were drawn into that bond with God which was the *covenant*, and became God's special people.

As the years passed they gradually deepened their awareness of what this God is like, and the prophets articulated this awareness so beautifully in passages like the following:

> **For the mountains may depart and the hills be removed, but my steadfast love shall not depart from you, and my covenant of peace shall not be removed, says the Lord, who has compassion on you.** (Isaiah 54:10)

Or again:

> But Zion said, 'The Lord has forsaken me, my Lord has forgotten me.' Can a woman forget her nursing child, or show no compassion for the child of her womb? Even these may forget, yet I will not forget you. See, I have inscribed you on the palms of my hands; your walls are continually before me.
> (Isaiah 49:14-16)

And Jeremiah:

> I have loved you with an everlasting love; therefore I have continued my faithfulness to you. (31:3)

The best way to sum up such insights is to suggest that Israel came to know God as faithful and compassionate love, a wonderful and deeply perceptive understanding. Reflection on this covenant relationship and what it entailed, led Israel to understand the appropriate response in these familiar terms:

> Hear, O Israel: The Lord is our God, the Lord alone. You shall love the Lord your God with all your heart, and with all your soul, and with all your might.
> (Deut 6:4-5)

These words, used later in discussion by Jesus himself, became fundamental to the prayer life of the people as they expressed their commitment to God. There is something quite radical, absolute and all-embracing about such a response; it captures something of the uniqueness of the covenant relationship. Israel came to see herself as God's special people. They belonged to God in a unique way.

Alongside this awareness and experience of familiarity we find a sense of reverence, awe and wonder. This can be seen in a primitive way in the Exodus story, when the people are forbidden to set foot on Sinai, and in the kind of acknowledgement of God's destructive force which we encounter in some of the psalms. It is seen also in their awareness of God's otherness:

> For as the heavens are higher than the earth, so are
> my ways higher than your ways and my thoughts
> than your thoughts. (Isaiah 55:9)

Such awareness of God's otherness is expressed also in Israel's recognition that the covenant, their relationship with God, their familiarity is gratuitous, is pure gift. They are God's people not because of any merit of their own, any achievement or qualities, but simply as a result of God's loving and free choice, and His ongoing faithfulness to that choice, despite their failings. There is ongoing wonder at that.

> For you are a people holy to the Lord your God; the
> Lord your God has chosen you out of all the peoples
> on earth to be his people, his treasured possession.
> It was not because you were more numerous than
> any other people that the Lord set his heart on you
> and chose you - for you were the fewest of all
> peoples. It was because the Lord loved you and
> kept the oath that he swore to your ancestors, that
> the Lord has brought you out with a mighty hand,
> and redeemed you from the house of slavery, from
> the hand of Pharaoh king of Egypt. Know therefore
> that the Lord your God is God, the faithful God who
> maintains covenant loyalty with those who love him
> and keep his commandments, to a thousand
> generations. (Deut 7:6-9)

The people are aware that they have been called to walk on holy ground, a place of love and wonder, of closeness and reverence.

NEW TESTAMENT

In the New Testament, the time of the new covenant established in the death and resurrection of Jesus, the age of the Spirit's outpouring, we again find that the closeness, the wonder, the giftedness, are powerfully present, but there are new ways of expressing this.

Early in John's Gospel there is an encounter between Jesus and Nicodemus, one of the Jewish religious leaders, a man who is aware that Jesus must have come from God. Jesus tells him of the need to be born again, born from above, born of water and Spirit. The dialogue becomes discourse as Jesus develops his teaching.

> And just as Moses lifted up the serpent in the wilderness, so must the Son of Man be lifted up, that whoever believes in him may have eternal life. For God so loved the world that he gave his only Son, so that everyone who believes in him may not perish but may have eternal life. Indeed, God did not send the Son into the world to condemn the world, but in order that the world might be saved through him. (John 3:14-17)

This extract contains the most celebrated expression of the Fourth Gospel, which sums up the whole Christian message of salvation. It is the Gospel in a nutshell. Behind everything stands the love of God, his free initiative and gift. The outcome of God's love is articulated in parallel sentences. God gives/sends His Son, His only Son. That giving/sending is for the benefit of the whole wide world. The purpose of that giving/sending is expressed twice, negatively and positively. It is that believers should not perish, or be destroyed or be judged (condemned); rather that they should have *eternal life*, be saved.

Rather than use the terms kingdom or salvation, John prefers *eternal life* (17 times). This is not to be understood mainly as everlasting life, a kind of life which starts only when normal earthly life ends in death. It is a qualitatively different kind of life, the life which pertains to the *above*, the heavenly realm; it is the life of God. It does therefore have an everlasting dimension. But the Fourth Evangelist stresses that *eternal life* is not a future dream only; it is a present reality. Already, now, believers come to share the life of the beyond. And death cannot snuff out this quality of life. It continues through death and reaches fulfilment beyond the grave. The Prologue states that *to those who did accept him he gave power to become children of God.*[1] We become God's children, we are caught up in God's life, through baptism, through birth by water and Spirit. And this new dimension of life becomes possible through the *uplifting* of Jesus, through his death and exaltation/glorification.

54

[1] 1:12-13

Paul too proclaims that the gift of the Spirit in baptism establishes a new relationship with God. He speaks of our being adopted as children, able to address God as *Abba! Father!*[2] He uses that distinctive and intimate title used by Jesus himself. The Spirit gift also draws us into a deep relationship with Christ; Paul frequently describes this as *being in Christ*.

The depth of our closeness with God is breathtaking. The giftedness of what has happened is powerfully highlighted in the letter to the Ephesians. Here we are invited to awe and wonder within the relationship of oneness.

> **So then, remember that you Gentiles by birth..... were at that time without Christ, being aliens from the commonwealth of Israel, and strangers to the covenants of promise, having no hope and without God in the world. But now in Christ Jesus you who once were far off have been brought near by the blood of Christ.** (Eph 2:11-13)

CONCLUSION

The New Testament, then, offers a more remarkable way of expressing that basic idea from the initial Moses passage. We are invited to walk on Holy Ground; we live and move and have our being in the heart of God. We are at home in God. As God's children, we share God's life. I think we need to allow this to sink in, to soak in, to permeate our being. Its implications are immense. It means that every aspect of our lives is drawn into the circle of God's love. There is nothing *ordinary* any more. All our activities, be they humdrum and mundane, or exciting and creative, have a new dimension, for they are caught up in our relationship with God - washing up, gardening, playing games, preparing lectures or classes, mending drains, marking books, sitting at traffic lights, practising the guitar - everything now has enormous significance, for all takes place on Holy Ground.

It is here that we find the source of that joy and optimism characteristic of Salesian spirituality. Don Bosco's Oratory was a *place of enjoyment*, and this is a model for all Salesian educational establishments. Salesians should be cheerful folk, radiating joy. But this joy is not champagne fizz, superficial exuberance and noise, raucous laughter on tap. Nor is it an expression of naïve unreality. We are aware of life's problems, difficulties and trials; we are aware of our own weaknesses, poverty and inadequacies; we are aware of the

[2] Gal 4:4; Rom 8:14

shortcomings of our Church and Congregation; we are aware of the weaknesses of our young people. We are in touch with the many challenges surrounding us. We do not deny the reality of sin.

Our serenity, peace and joy, are rooted in our knowledge that we have been embraced by the God of faithful love, that we have been saved by Jesus. We know that we already share God's life. We entrust ourselves into the hands of God, and we entrust those whom we seek to serve, and the various situations we find ourselves in. We believe that nothing can separate us or them from the love of God in Jesus. Because of the resurrection of Jesus, we believe that love is stronger than evil. We believe in God's will and power to use us and our giftedness, despite our fragility. We can believe in people, especially the young, with their enormous potential for good. We can live with a positive attitude, in gentle optimism and strong hope.

One of the lasting legacies of St Francis de Sales is his teaching that all are called to holiness, and that holiness has to do with the fulfilling of the duties of one's ordinary way of life, insights revisited by the Second Vatican Council. In his day Don Bosco placed this fundamental life challenge before young people, with remarkable results. He insisted that they were not to engage in excessive penances, long fasts, hours of prayer. Rather, holiness consisted in being always cheerful, doing their daily tasks as well as possible, and helping their companions. The potential within the ordinary is quite extraordinary.

I must admit that the language of holiness, and the accompanying baggage resulting from much religious art and hagiography, fails to set the adrenalin flowing. Another way of approaching the issue, which I find more attractive, is suggested by John V Taylor.[3] He prefers to speak of aliveness. We are called to become fully alive, and aliveness implies awareness and responsiveness.

The Spirit quietly works to bring us more fully alive, making us more aware of the beauty of the natural world in which we live, more sensitive to the richness, originality and mystery of the human beings whom we encounter, more in touch with what is going on within us, more open to the splendour and tragedy of human experience, and more interested in its many facets and shades, more alert to human need at all levels of society. The Spirit prompts us to respond appropriately. The Spirit awakens us to God's presence in and through all this.

3 See J V Taylor, *A Matter of Life and Death* (London, SCM 1986), p 17-31.

Taking off One's Sandals

Going back to the Moses story, I would like to pick up the detail about his being told to take off his sandals. Where does that fit in to what I have been saying? It was for Moses the symbol of his awareness that he was on Holy Ground. Going barefoot was a sign of reverence and wonder within familiarity. And for us too it symbolises our acknowledging and appreciating God's closeness, our belonging to him, our being caught up in the mystery of his love and presence, all the time, everywhere.

The problem for me is that I am inclined to forget. So I tend to tramp across God's garden, walk on Holy Ground, with clogs on, or heavy boots. I can lose sight of the fact that I am on Holy Ground. I travel up and down motorways and get snarled up in traffic jams. I organise and run lots of meetings. I prepare lectures and talks. I do cooking, and washing up. I get involved in building plans and projects, become busier and busier, feel more and more pressurised, as the phone keeps ringing and people knock at my door, and... We all probably experience the same kind of thing with different examples! I can get so caught up in it all that I overlook or forget the fact that all this is taking place on Holy Ground, and that I am in the heart of God. I've neglected to take off my sandals. I have lost the contemplative dimension of my Christian existence. That is sad. It is also foolish of me.

There is another dimension of this image of Holy Ground in connection with Salesian spirituality. This combination of reverence and familiarity has bearing on our relationships with others. This can apply at all levels – in family and community, church, school, club, workplace, or ministry, formal or casual. When I encounter another person, I am approaching Holy Ground, the sacredness of mystery, the uniqueness and richness of human personhood. Each person is original, unrepeatable, and has their own life and faith journey, their own history. Each is a person deeply loved and valued by God, always precious in God's sight, caught up in God's saving design, in the embrace of God's compassionate and faithful love. On that ground I must walk without sandals. In many of the Gospel narratives I sense the reverence of Jesus for those he meets. Often this is expressed in the gesture of touching them into wholeness and healing.

As I look into my own life I can see that I so easily miss the deeper dimension of the person before me. I forget the God-context in which each encounter, whether it is a daily or frequent encounter, or a one-off meeting, takes place. No encounter is ever ordinary. Every meeting takes place in the heart of God. One of the sad aspects and great impoverishments of society today is the lack of respect and reverence.

I know that this contemplative approach is not easy. It can be difficult to take off one's sandals in the presence of people who are awkward, fussy, demanding, difficult, troublesome, ill-mannered, impatient... I'm not starry eyed! And yet, though difficult, this is basic to the Salesian way. If we are not careful, we can find ourselves trampling clumsily on people, insensitive and uncaring, oblivious to their pains and problems, unappreciative of their giftedness, lacking in warmth and acceptance. I firmly believe that the basis of any relationship, be it friendship, professional collaboration, Christian community, ministry, is reverence. It is the ability to kneel barefoot in wonder, to perceive the in-depth dimension of each individual, to see the person in the sacred space of God's loving presence, to be aware of mystery. Without reverence there can be no real love.

Obviously, reverence for others and reverence for God go hand in hand. They are complementary expressions of a contemplative soul, a person walking barefooted on Holy Ground.

PRAYER SUGGESTION

Spend some time soaking in the truth of God's love, God's invitation to spend my life on Holy Ground. Allow the realisation of the immense value of the ordinary things in life to blossom. How can this make a difference? How do I express my reverence for God, for other people, for the world in which I live?

CHAPTER SEVEN - PRAYER AND ACTION

One of the challenges of Salesian spirituality is to maintain a balance between prayer and action, between a praying heart and busy hands, between union with God and self-gift to others. In this chapter I would like to share with you some scriptural reflections on the relationship between the contemplative and active dimensions of Salesian spirituality, a relationship sometimes described as the *grace of unity*. This I propose to do in two stages: firstly, to consider the theme in Mark, and then examine Luke's presentation.

MARK

As the starting point I would like to use a favourite passage of mine from the opening section of Mark's Gospel. It is, I believe, another extract which could be termed *characteristically Salesian*, Mark 1:29-39.

It is often stated by the scholars that in the early part of his narrative the Evangelist Mark, after the call of the first four disciples, condenses within the framework of a single *model* day several typical aspects of the mission of Jesus. This serves as a kind of preview and summary of the whole ministry. Mark describes how Jesus goes along to the synagogue on the Sabbath. There he begins to teach, with remarkable authority and effectiveness, and he performs a dramatic exorcism. In fact, Mark repeatedly presents the mission of Jesus under this twofold rubric of preaching and exorcising. When the service is over, Jesus goes along to Simon's house and heals Simon's mother-in-law.

After this comes a scene bustling with activity and excitement, as, when the Sabbath sun has set, and the people can do so without breaking the Law, they come thronging at the door of the house where Jesus is staying, bringing their sick and disabled, noisily crying for healing, and making heart-rending demands on Jesus' compassion. He responds with cures and exorcisms, loosening evil's hold on their lives.

Then the scene changes, and there is a striking contrast. The atmosphere is different now. The crowds have dispersed and Jesus is alone. Instead of the heat and dust and clamour, there is the cool stillness of the late night. Hectic activity is replaced by silence, stillness and prayer.

This long silence is broken and the prayer disturbed by the sudden arrival of Simon Peter and the others who have tracked Jesus down. Simon brusquely informs him that the people are all looking for him. They seem to want him for his cures and wonders. Simon and the rest of the disciples wish Jesus to stay in the area and capitalise on his soaring popularity, in the glow of which, doubtless, they would enjoy basking. Jesus senses in such enthusiasm the danger of his being misunderstood, and so he resists their request and pressurising. He replies:

> **Let us go elsewhere, to the neighbouring country**
> **towns, so that I can proclaim the message there**
> **too, because that is why I came.** (1:38)

The activity and restless movement commence again, as Jesus went all through Galilee, preaching in their synagogues and driving out devils.[1]

This Markan extract illustrates the fascinating interplay between prayer and ministry in the life of Jesus. I believe that by locating this incident at the outset of the ministry, Mark intends us to understand that the secret of Jesus and his mission is to be found in these periods of solitary prayer and reflection. In a book which I read some time ago, I came across a beautiful and insightful description of the prayer of Jesus as *listening to the Father's love*. Awareness of that love for him, that unique love, as expressed in the baptism experience,[2] enables Jesus to address God as *Abba, Father*, which he explicitly does in Gethsemane.[3] It enables him to experience God's intimacy and care, to know God as compassion, acceptance, forgiveness and unconditional love. It is here that he is nearest to the Father's heart, as John would phrase it.[4] It is, I believe, this knowledge and experience which gives Jesus that assurance and freedom so characteristic of him. Awareness of the Father's love for the world impels Jesus to reach out in healing compassion and self-giving service. Mark's careful structuring of this section, with prayer at the centre, flanked by the two scenes of activity, underlines the ebb and flow movement between prayer and action.

[1] Mk 1:39
[2] 1:11
[3] 14:36
[4] 1:18

The Evangelist considered this to be fundamental to the life and mission of Jesus. This must also be the basic pattern of our existence as disciples of Jesus. It is the paradigm which enables Salesians to follow Don Bosco, as contemplatives in action.

The core of the prayer which, according to Luke, Jesus taught his disciples at their request is: *Father, your kingdom come.*5 This phrase captures both the intimate relationship between Jesus and the Father, and Jesus' commitment to his mission. *Abba* entails *Yes.* The deeper that love experience, the greater the surrender in loving trust to the mission entrusted to him. We are invited to make that prayer our own; we are drawn into that relationship, called to participate in that mission. Again relationship and mission belong together. I think it was Sobrino, the Jesuit theologian, who defined obedience as discerning the demands of love and responding positively.

The Salesian Constitutions put this very well: *In praying, the Salesian community responds to God's call; it deepens its awareness of its intimate and living relationship with God, and of its saving mission.*6 They go on to recall how Don Bosco lived an experience of humble, trusting and apostolic prayer, in which praying and living were spontaneously united. *Each one needs to express his own personal and heartfelt way of being a son of God, expressing his gratitude, telling God about his yearnings and his concerns in the apostolate.*7

LUKE

The importance of integrating the contemplative and active dimensions of our response to God, as disciples of Jesus, is illustrated in an interesting and challenging way by Luke in his handling of the tradition about the great commandment:

> **You must love the Lord your God with all your heart, with all your soul, with all your strength, and with all your mind, and your neighbour as yourself.**
> (10:27)

In his narrative the lawyer's question about inheriting eternal life occurs soon after Jesus has resolutely turned his face towards Jerusalem. This central section of Luke's Gospel contains much of his special material, and presents key aspects

---

5 Lk 11:2
6 Constitution 85
7 Constitution 93

of Christian discipleship, as Luke understood it. Jesus persuades the lawyer to answer his own question.

Whereas in Mark there are two commandments - love of God and love of neighbour - in Luke's formulation there is a single unified love command, with a twin focus. The meaning of the commandment is then illustrated by the parable of the Good Samaritan and the parabolic narrative of Martha and Mary. Usually these are treated separately, but structurally they belong together.

THE PARABLE OF THE GOOD SAMARITAN (10: 29-37)

The lawyer in the narrative finds it hard to let go of the idea of *earning* eternal life with which he has begun his encounter with Jesus. He continues to press for answers, to assert himself and regain the initiative. Jesus has forced him to answer his own question, and challenged him to live by what he knows. So he next attempts to clarify the meaning of the Law by seeking a definition of the term *neighbour*, or a clear delineation of the limits of his responsibility. Usually, the Jews considered as belonging to the category of neighbour, fellow Jews, resident aliens, and proselytes. There were others classified as non-neighbour, and there were exceptions within the community. With a clear list in mind, the lawyer would be able to tick off those loved, and feel justified in being able to say: *I have done it*. To his question: *And who is my neighbour?* Jesus replies with the famous parable.

The Story

A man, whom we presume to be a Jew, is travelling the lonely seventeen-mile descent from Jerusalem to Jericho. The terrain is rough and rocky, and provides ideal cover for robbers, organised bands of highwaymen, and it offers ready escape routes too. The man is ambushed, beaten up, stripped and left half dead. The detail that he is stripped and unconscious is essential to create the tension at the heart of the drama. He cannot identify himself; nor can his identity easily be ascertained by another. Conversation is impossible, and his accent or dialect would betray his origins. Any distinctive garb has been removed: he therefore belongs to no ethnic group or religious community. He is simply a human being in need.

A priest happens to pass that way. Many of the priestly families resided in Jericho; the priests would go up to Jerusalem when their turn for ministry came around. Presumably this one is returning from one of his two weeks of service. Since he is a member of the upper class, he is probably riding. This is also demanded by the structure of the parable, for he and the Samaritan are in parallel. He steers his mount to the far side of the road and passes by.

Several motives are put forward to explain his passing by. Fear of a trap or ambush; unwillingness to get involved; heartlessness. Many scholars opt for his theological and legalistic mentality, his fear of incurring ritual defilement. The priest is unable to identify the victim securely as a Jew; he may be dead. Contact would in either case defile a priest, at least according to the Sadducee interpretation. If defiled, he would not be able to officiate at services, or wear phylacteries; nor could he collect, distribute or eat tithes. His family and servants would suffer as a consequence. To incur defilement would be a great humiliation for a priest, especially so soon after finishing his term of office. Purification would take a week, would be financially costly, and would entail returning to the East Gate and standing amongst other *unclean*. It is better to maintain status and righteousness within the system and the supporting community than to reach out to one in need.

The next person on the scene is a Levite. The Levites too formed a privileged group. They were cultic officials involved in Temple liturgy; they also exercised a policing role. This man would not be bound by as many regulations as the priest; he was required to observe ritual cleanness only whilst on duty. So he approaches, probably takes a closer look, and decides against helping. In his case the motive would not be fear of defilement. He could be walking, and fears to linger because of danger of the robbers. He would probably be aware of the priest ahead, since it was possible to see a good distance; if the priest were mounted, he could have overtaken him earlier. Perhaps he argues that it isn't his duty to help, since the priest has not done so. To do so could be construed as a criticism of the priest's conduct. Although professionally a religious man, there is nothing in his orientation which moves him to help.

A third man reaches the scene. Perhaps Jesus' original hearers, not adverse to a little spicy anti-clericalism, expected this protagonist in the drama to be a Jewish layman. This would be the natural sequence. To their shock and dismay, Jesus chooses as hero a Samaritan. There had been centuries of animosity between Jews and Samaritans. The Samaritans had opposed the restoration of Jerusalem after the exile, and had later helped the Syrians against the Jews. In 128 BC the Jewish High Priest burned the Samaritan Temple on Mount Gerizim. In Jesus' time hostility had intensified because of an incident in which the Samaritans had defiled the temple and prevented the celebration of Passover by strewing dead men's bones there. They were cursed in the synagogue worship; there was a prayer that they would be refused eternal life. So Jesus was really rocking the boat, chancing his arm, stirring and exposing the deepest hatreds and emotions and religiously institutionalised prejudices of his audience. It must have taken great courage to make a despised, mistrusted, heretical, as-bad-as-Gentile Samaritan appear as morally superior to religious Jews, and as exemplar of the true fulfilment of the Law! Jesus raises the very basic question about the people's understanding of God and the nature of God's approval. The Samaritans were hostile to Jesus' own ministry in 9:53, a detail which reflects his magnanimity.

A Samaritan too was subject to the Law, and risked contamination. He too would risk attack from robbers if he lingered, especially if carrying merchandise; and he wasn't a man of the cloth. He would doubtless be aware that the other two had ignored a man who was probably a fellow Jew, and so might wonder why he should get involved.

But, *when he saw him, he was moved to compassion.* Compassion is the turning point of the narrative, a compassion which finds immediate, concrete, practical expression. *Compassion is the bridge between simply looking on injured and half-dead fellow human beings and entering their world with saving care.*[8]

To begin with he renders first aid. He cleans and softens the wounds with oil, disinfects them with wine, and bandages them up. The word order is unusual. Perhaps it is meant to recall God's binding of wounds.[9] The second stage of the rescue is that he provides transport. He may have had several donkeys. It is not clear whether the two ride the same animal or whether the Samaritan puts the victim on his own mount, and then leads the animal as would a servant. In Palestine the social distinction between the rider and the one leading the animal is important. He takes him to an inn, presumably in Jericho, and remains overnight ministering to his needs. This is a marvellous act of self-giving love, easy for us to overlook. In that culture, blood revenge was deeply rooted. If someone is hurt and the assailant cannot be found, anyone, even if only

64

8 J R Donahue, *The Gospel in Parable*, p 132 See also K E Bailey, *Poet and Peasant*, and *Through Peasant Eyes*, p 33-56.
9 Jer 30:17; Hos 6

remotely connected, could suffer. So, in taking him to Jericho, he runs the risk of the community blaming him and attacking him, as an irrational group response, especially as he belonged to a minority group. Caution would suggest that, at the very most, he should take him to the inn and then disappear. In staying around, in offering to return later, he displays great courage. What a price he is prepared to pay to complete the act of compassion!

Thirdly, to complete the balanced framework of the parable, he compensates for the robbers. They rob, leave, abandon. He pays, leaves, promises to return. Innkeepers had an unsavoury reputation for dishonesty and violence. If simply left there, the man on awaking would not be able to pay the bill since he had been robbed, and so could be arrested for debt. The Samaritan's advance payment, and promise of settling further expenses with the innkeeper on his return, guarantees the man's freedom and security. There is no mention of his being reimbursed.

The story is an amazing delineation by Jesus of the meaning of compassion. Note the cost in time, effort, convenience, and finance. Not to mention personal danger, a cost completely disregarded. Utter self-forgetfulness, generous attention, service far beyond the call of duty, thoughtful concern and foresight. The contrast between the action of the hated Samaritan and the inaction of the respected Jewish religious elite is quite stunning. *Jesus deliberately shocks the lawyer by forcing him to consider the possibility that a semi-pagan foreigner might know more about the love of God than a devout Jew blinded by preoccupation with pettifogging rules.*[10]

The Sequel
The lawyer's initial question sought a definition of neighbour, a list of categories which would fall under this rubric. He hopes that by fulfilling the requirements of the list, a prescriptive law, he will be able to earn eternal life for himself. How many people have I to love in order to earn righteousness by my own efforts?

Jesus concludes the parable by rephrasing the initial question: which of the three proved himself to be neighbour? Jesus is not primarily interested in responding directly to the definition-seeking question, but in exploring the nature of neighbourliness. The commandment had been quoted as *love neighbour*. For Jesus it is the verb that matters. The lawyer's answer, which

---

[10] G B Caird, *Luke*, p 148-149.

avoids the naming of the Samaritan, is again correct, *the one who shows kindness.* Neighbour has become subject rather than object. *Neighbour is a way of being in the world, it is a way of relating to other people and to God.*[11] But Jesus has, in fact, answered the original question; neighbour means any human being in need, beyond ethnic and religious restrictions.

The encounter closes in parallel with the earlier question with a further challenge from Jesus: *Go, and you do likewise.* And of course the lawyer cannot, the standard is too high. To become neighbour to anyone in need, to reach out in costly compassion to all people, even enemies, without any limits is a demanding ideal. And the verb means *keep on doing it*, make treating everyone with compassion a way of life. Though we cannot achieve it, the standard remains. And in the end, eternal life will be God's gift. *The parable summons us to a solidarity with suffering men and women and tells us that such solidarity can come only when we can acquire hearts of flesh and a compassionate vision...*[12] This forces us back up the mountain to pray, to listen to the Father's compassion.

MARTHA AND MARY (10:38-42)

In Luke's mind the story of the two sisters, Martha and Mary, which is not found in the other Gospels, is coupled with the parable of the Good Samaritan. Both illustrate the two aspects of the one commandment of love. It is also an instance of Luke's tendency to juxtapose two narratives, in one the principal protagonist is a man, in the other a woman. He is a forerunner in the call for equal opportunities and collaborative ministry.

In the course of Jesus' journey to Jerusalem he reaches a village, and is in need of hospitality. Martha makes him welcome in her home. She appears to be the mistress of the household, and busily gets involved in preparing a rather elaborate meal. In John 12 it is Martha who prepares the meal. Mary, her sister, *seated herself at the Lord's feet and stayed there listening to his words.* She adopts the normal posture of a disciple, and is clearly keen to listen and to learn from the Teacher. She is attentive to his word, a key motif for this Evangelist. Jesus, far from shrinking from this, as most rabbis would have done, encourages her. This is another example of his freedom with regard to social and religious convention in his treatment of women, and of his advancing their status.

[11] D McBride, *The Gospel of Luke*, p 139.
[12] J R Donahue, *The Gospel in Parable*, p 134.

Martha has a problem. The pressure of hospitality, as she understands it, prevents her from listening, which she doubtless would have appreciated and enjoyed. She is *distracted by all the serving*. The verb means pulled or dragged away, distracted.[13] There is too much to do. She probably feels rather peeved that she has been left to do everything herself, and maybe thinks her sister is being rather selfish. Perhaps she is a little disappointed that Jesus does not seem to notice. So she attempts to enlist his support. She evinces a slightly confrontational attitude. One might detect a touch of resentment in her voice, a tone of accusation against her sister: *Tell her to come and lend a hand.* She ought not to have asked a guest to become involved in a family dispute.

As is generally the case in the Gospel narrative, Jesus resists the pressure to intervene.[14] He is not unsympathetic to her plight and her problem, and her feelings of annoyance; but he insists on priorities. There is great affection in his voice as he indicates the real issue.

> **Martha, Martha, you are fretting and fussing about so many things.** (10:41)

The first verb means to be anxious, to be unduly concerned. Anxiety usually has a negative connotation, implying a lack of trust in the presence and power of God; it can inhibit the growth of the word.[15] The second verb means to be troubled, distracted, to create an uproar. Martha, then, is too troubled and anxious; she is over-concerned. She is losing the right perspective. It is not really necessary to *go over the top*, to prepare such an elaborate menu. Perhaps she could cut back a little, and thus have time to listen.

There are two aspects to discipleship: there is service and kindness and practical living; and there is listening to Jesus, hearing the word of the Lord. As Caird puts it so well: Martha *has not yet learned that unselfishness, service, and even sacrifice can be spoiled by self-concern and self-pity, that good works which are not self-forgetful can become a misery to the doer and a tyranny to others.*[16]

> **Mary has chosen the good portion, which shall not be taken away from her.** (10:42)

[13] See 1 Cor 7:35
[14] 12:13
[15] 8:14
[16] G B Caird, *Luke*, p 150.

After the story of the Samaritan, the reply of Jesus is surprising. It has also proved problematic, as the manuscript variations testify. The good or better part, portion, course or dish (a little wordplay is evident here), the thing which is most essential, the right choice, is to make space for Jesus, and to listen. Such listening shapes and enlivens our active caring. Johnson writes that the one thing necessary for hospitality is attention to the guest. *If the guest is a prophet, the appropriate reception is listening to God's word!*[17] In the scale of values, it is listening to the word which has priority.

CONCLUSION

To love God with whole heart and mind and the neighbour as one's self demands both compassionate and effective entry into the world of the neighbour as well as undistracted attentiveness to the word of the Lord. Far from exalting one mode of discipleship above the other, the two narratives say that one cannot authentically exist without the other.[18] For Luke it is important both to hear and to do.*[19]*

For Salesians, there is, I think, a danger of being too busy being Samaritans to listen to the word with silent attentiveness, to go to the mountain of prayer. Often our busy-ness is tinged with over-anxiety, inducing stress and tension. In some cases one can detect symptoms of workaholism, incipient or verging on the chronic. This can entail a blurring of perspective, a loss of true focus. When there are clashes of priorities, it tends to be prayer which is jettisoned. Without times of prayer in which we listen to God's love, our apostolic ventures can become jobs or careers rather than ministries. We run the risk of building our own kingdoms rather than that of Jesus. Values, other than those of the Gospel, can influence our decisions and actions. Selfishness, individualism and pragmatism and the seeking of success, instead of the Spirit, can determine our discernment.

PRAYER SUGGESTION

We can reflect on a typical day or week and examine the rhythm of our lives, our integration of prayer and action. It could be useful to spend some time pondering the parable which Jesus told, in an effort to understand the demands of compassion. We could attempt to wear the sandals of Martha, then of Mary and finally of Jesus in the scene in the house, and try to enter into their feelings.

68

[17] L T Johnson, *Luke*, p 175.
[18] J R Donahue, *The Gospel in Parable*, p 136-137.
[19] 8:21; 11:28

CHAPTER EIGHT - MISSION

The Salesian Constitutions state that The Salesian vocation places us at the heart of the Church and puts us entirely at the service of her mission.[1] In this chapter I would like to reflect on the topic of mission, using the Gospels as a launching pad. I propose to do so firstly by examining Jesus' sense of mission, and then by exploring various models of mission which the Evangelists and Paul provide.

A SENSE OF MISSION

I'd like to begin with Easter Day. The various resurrection narratives or appearance stories, have many similar structural characteristics. They follow a basic pattern, a kind of template. A key element of that format is the commissioning of the recipients by the Risen Jesus, his sending them on mission.

In John's description of Easter Day, for instance, Jesus appears to his fearful disciples as they cower in the upper room with the doors firmly locked. He wishes them *Peace*, and then tells them:

> 'As the Father has sent me, so I send you.' When he had said this, he breathed on them and said to them, 'Receive the Holy Spirit.' (John 20:21-22)

Matthew, who follows the Galilee appearance tradition, couches the commissioning in rather different terms:

> And Jesus came and said to them, 'All authority in heaven and on earth has been given to me. Go therefore and make disciples of all nations, baptising them in the name of the Father and of the Son and of the Holy Spirit, and teaching them to obey everything that I have commanded you. And remember, I am with you always, to the end of the age.' (Matthew 28:18-20)

[1] Constitution 6

Magdalen, in John's Gospel, is told not to cling to Jesus, but to go to the brothers and tell them that he is ascending to his Father and theirs, his God and theirs. In Luke the disciples are sent to preach forgiveness to the nations.

The transformation of failed disciples into apostles is quite remarkable. Their new found sense of mission, which results from their encounter with the Risen Jesus, mirrors the sense of mission which is one of the salient characteristics of the Gospel portrait of Jesus himself during his ministry.

I'm always impressed by the strength of that fundamental conviction of his *being sent*. I believe that this conviction arose out of his confidence that he stood in a specially intimate relationship with God, whom he addressed as *Abba, Father*. Jesus was convinced that he experienced the power of God's Spirit working effectively in him, and through him, in his exorcisms and healings and *mighty works*. He was conscious of his authority. This is seen, for instance, in the two phrases characteristic of his preaching style: his frequent use of *Amen* to preface an assertion, guaranteeing its truth; and his emphatic *but I say to you*, as he sets aside the authority of Moses and the Law in favour of his own teaching. Without having recourse to precedent or experts, Jesus claims to know the heart and mind of God directly. His consciousness of authority is also seen in the demands which he believed he could make of others. Jesus believed that through his words and deeds the Kingdom of God was being established, and that his mission, his life's work, was bound up with this.

It is the Fourth Evangelist who develops this theme most fully. More than forty times Jesus articulates his conviction of *being sent*, or *having come*. We find on his lips expressions like these:

> **My food is to do the will of the one who sent me, and to complete his work.** (4:34)

> **I have come from heaven not to do my own will, but to do the will of him who sent me.** (6:38)

And his last words: *It is finished*, refer to the completion of the task which he had been given by the Father, the fulfilment of his mission, *mission accomplished*. For John, Jesus is totally referred to the Father, and totally taken up with mission.

The two go together. It's like the two sides of the same coin. The connection is made in his prayer, which has become ours: *Father, may your kingdom come.*

As disciples of Jesus, we are caught up into his mission. We are people who are *sent*; this is integral to our Christian identity. One of the salient features of Don Bosco was his conviction that God had chosen him for a specific mission in life, that he was sent to the young. In the early days when things were going badly, he confided to a friend, Carlo Gastini: *They are all leaving me. But I have God with me - what is there to fear? The work is His, not mine. He will take care of it and carry it forward.* On another occasion he reflected: *It was the Lord who began it all, who directed all things and gave them growth. As the years roll by, God will uphold them and bring them to a successful ending.*[2] Don Rua[3] asserts that Don Bosco *took no step, he said no word, he took up no task that was not directed to the saving of the young... Truly, the only concern of his heart was for souls.*

MODELS OF MISSION

When I think of mission in my own life, I find that I have two preoccupations. The first is to bear in mind that mission is not simply about doing, about action, about ministry, about work. It is about being and becoming. We are to witness to a certain way of being human. The second is to avoid missing the wood for the trees. It's so easy to get bogged down in the nitty-gritty of ministry, to be caught up in the nuts and bolts of apostolate, to lose sight of the broader canvass.

There is a story told of an incident which happened during the construction of Durham Cathedral a thousand or so years ago. The abbot of the adjacent monastery was showing an illustrious friend around the construction site. As they wandered around looking at this, admiring that, his friend approached one of the many stonemasons, and asked him what he was doing. He looked up, and swallowing a couple of north-eastern expletives, replied: *I'm chipping stone,* in a tone which implied, *What do you think I'm doing?* The abbot and his friend moved on to the south side overlooking the River Wear, and the visitor repeated his question to another stonemason. This fellow looked up at him with a twinkle in his eye and replied: *I'm building a cathedral.*

Often, I know, I become a stone chipper, too narrowly and busily focussed –

2 E Ceria, *The Biographical Memoirs of Saint John Bosco* (New Rochelle, Salesiana Publishers 1980), vol 12, p 64.
3 Don Rua was the first successor to Don Bosco.

preparing lectures and handouts for College, agendas and reports for meetings, fitting appointments into a full diary, sorting out retreat talks, bombing up and down traffic-filled motorways, setting dining room tables and tidying up. There's no cathedral in view. So I believe that it is helpful to return to the scriptures for orientation, for vaster vistas, to find my roots again. There are in the New Testament a number of strands or patterns of thought, a number of models, which I believe can underpin and enlighten our understanding of Salesian mission, and give it direction.[4]

TO GIVE LIGHT AND LIFE

Since we have just been referring to the Fourth Gospel, we can launch our exploration there. One of the ways in which John portrays the mission of Jesus is through the imagery of light and life. Jesus comes in order to be the light of the world, the unique and authoritative revealer of the Father, and he is sent to give life to the world, life in all its fullness.[5]

Much of John's rich symbolism suggests this revelation motif. In the context of the feast of Tabernacles, when the city at night was bathed in candlelight, Jesus claims that it is he who is the light of the world.[6] The subsequent healing of the man born blind and his journey into the vision of faith illustrate the truth and significance of this claim.[7] In the dialogue with the Samaritan woman he offers living water, which is often interpreted as meaning revelation and teaching, as well as referring to the Spirit.[8] Jesus is the bread of life, which in the earlier part of the famous discourse is generally thought to refer primarily to revelation.[9] In the Supper Discourse he calls his disciples *friends*, because he has disclosed to them everything he has learned from the Father.[10] At the conclusion of his final prayer Jesus claims to have revealed to *his own* the Father's name, the very being of God.[11] He is able to make God known because he has come from God, remains close to the Father's heart,[12] and is taught by the Father.[13]

Jesus, when speaking to Nicodemus, explains that God in his love has sent him into the world so that believers may have eternal life.[14] In elucidating his claim to be the Good Shepherd he states that he has come so that the sheep *may have life and have it to the full*.[15] This aspect of his mission is illustrated by three signs: the cure of the centurion's son,[16] the healing of the cripple by the Bethesda pool,[17] and especially by the raising of Lazarus.[18] Jesus is, in fact, the resurrection and the life.[19]

[4] This is a slightly adapted version of a section in *Scripture, Sacraments, Spirituality* p 52-60, printed with permission.

[5] 10:10	[9] 6:25-51	[13] 8:26,40	[17] 5:1f
[6] 8:12	[10] 15:15	[14] 3:16-17	[18] 11:1f
[7] 9:1-38	[11] 17:26	[15] 10:10	[19] 11:25
[8] 4:10	[12] 1:18	[16] 4:46f	

As Jesus was sent by the Father, so we his disciples are sent, empowered by the Spirit.[20] We are sent to witness to, reveal and make known the love of God, which is the truth that sets people free.[21] We do this through our words; we communicate it especially through the quality of our love and service. And we are to promote, foster, enable aliveness in all its dimensions. This is, I believe, an inspiring and vibrant way of understanding our mission.

TO GATHER INTO UNITY

A second Johannine model emphasises the movement towards unity, the gathering into one. This topic is first broached in the discourse about shepherding, an image deeply rooted in biblical tradition, as we have seen.[22] Jesus identifies himself as the Good Shepherd, who knows his sheep intimately and is concerned for them. In contrast to the hireling who, when danger looms, takes to flight to save his skin, Jesus is prepared to lay down his life for his sheep. He then continues:

> **I have other sheep that do not belong to this fold.**
> **I must bring them also, and they will listen to my**
> **voice. So there will be one flock, one shepherd.**
> (10:16)

This vision of a single flock under one shepherd, found earlier in the prophets,[23] implies that the love of Jesus unto death, and the abundant life which he has come to offer, are not restricted to the people of Israel. Others too will hear his voice. A new flock, a new community, comprising both Jew and Greek, will come into existence. This new unity reflects and is based on the oneness between Jesus and the Father.[24]

Later, as John's plot unfolds, the Jewish religious leaders, *the chief priests and Pharisees*, in the wake of the enthusiastic response to the raising of Lazarus, call a meeting at which Caiaphas, the High Priest at the time, presides. This is the Johannine equivalent of the Sanhedrin trial scene found in the Synoptic passion narratives, and omitted in the Johannine passion. In fact, the whole of John's Gospel is considered by many scholars as the trial of Jesus. The leaders are deeply disturbed by the large numbers rushing after Jesus; they are afraid that *everybody will believe in him*, and that this will result in the Romans taking decisive and destructive action against Temple and nation. At this point

[20] 20:21
[21] 8:32
[22] 10:1-38
[23] see Mic 5:3-5; Jer 3:15; 23:4-6; Ezek 34:23-24
[24] 10:15,18,30

Caiaphas disparagingly highlights their lack of perception, and indicates that:

> **You do not understand that it is better for you to have one man die for the people than to have the whole nation destroyed.** (11:50)

There is a touch of cynical pragmatism in Caiaphas' approach. Ironically, the phrasing suggests the thinking, current at the time, about the sacrifice of the Maccabaean martyrs, whose deaths saved Israel. The narrator continues:

> **He did not say this on his own, but being high priest that year he prophesied that Jesus was about to die for the nation, and not for the nation only, but to gather into one the dispersed children of God.** (11:51-52)

The comment underlines that the effects of Jesus' death will be felt beyond the confines of Israel. Others, right across the world, who are also children of God, will be drawn in, *gathered* to form a new people, a new community.

Later in the narrative, after Jesus' entry into Jerusalem, the Pharisees note with some discouragement that *the whole world has gone after him*.[25] This comment is followed by the arrival of some Greeks who have come to look for Jesus. Their request to see him, conveyed by Andrew and Philip, is taken as the sign that the *hour* has now finally come, the hour of the glorification of the Son of man. There follows a scene which is the Johannine equivalent of the Synoptic agony in Gethsemane. There is the terror and anguish, the prayer to the Father, the surrender to the Father's will. Then Jesus exclaims:

> **Now is the judgment of this world; now the ruler of this world will be driven out. And I, when I am lifted up from the earth, will draw all people to myself.** (12:31-32)

The *gathering* of all to Jesus is the purpose and result of his being *lifted up*, his being raised on the cross, which is also his exaltation.

Finally, there is the prayer of Jesus at the supper:

[25] 12:19

that they may all be one. As you, Father, are in me and I am in you, may they also be in us, so that the world may believe that you have sent me. (17:21)

This vision of unity is found also in the opening hymn of the letter to the Ephesians, a hymn frequently recited in the Church's Office. In this hymn, which some scholars think may have originated in a baptismal liturgy, we praise and thank our God and Father for choosing us, for accepting us, for forgiving us, for freely lavishing his gifts upon us. We thank him also for letting us know the mystery of God's purpose, his overarching plan, namely:

that he would bring everything together under Christ as head, everything in the heavens and everything on earth. (1:10 NJB)

The picture is that of the restoration of God's rule to the whole universe as well as humankind. For the author of this letter it is clear that the clearest symbol of such unifying is the breaking down of the barrier between Jew and Gentile.

But now in Christ Jesus you that used to be so far off have been brought close, by the blood of Christ. For he is the peace between us, and has made the two into one entity and broken down the barrier which used to keep them apart by destroying in his own person the hostility, that is, the Law of commandments with its decrees. His purpose in this was, by restoring peace, to create a single New Man out of the two of them, and through the cross, to reconcile them both to God in one Body; in his own person he killed the hostility. He came to bring the good news of peace to you who were far off and peace to those who were near. Through him, then, we both in the one Spirit have free access to the Father. (2:13-18 NJB)

The saving activity of Jesus is expressed in terms of a unifying which abolishes fundamental differences. In spatial terms the reconciliation obtained by Jesus' death is both horizontal and vertical. Through the gift of the Spirit all are drawn into equal relationship with God as Father, and incorporated into the one Christ, and thus brought into a new unity with one another across all divides. All are now the one people of God, the Church.

I have long felt drawn to this vision. I think that it was this passage which inspired Teilhard de Chardin, whom I admired in my student days. He envisaged the whole of creation as moving from chaos and utter disunity, moving upwards and inwards into greater unity. Christ is the rod or axis running through it all, drawing it together; and Christ is the climactic point to which this vast movement is directed.

At a personal level, a social or community level, a political level, a cosmic level, this model is extremely evocative. In this view of things, evil and sin can be seen in terms of existing disharmony, or the introduction of further disunity, or a falling back into dispersion and division, or a refusal to integrate, to grow into oneness, to advance to greater harmony. Mission, then, has to do with integrating and unifying, overcoming opposition and division, promoting what unites, fighting all that estranges and separates. For Teilhard, the energising force of this process is love.

What is also significant about this unity model of mission, is that such unity is the result of Jesus' death. This is evident in each of the passages which we have considered: the shepherd motif, the trial scene, the statement about being *lifted up*. This indicates that unity is the gift of God, but is also costly for those involved. It suggests that our participation in this mission will entail considerable dying, like the wheat grain.[26] For:

> **Whoever serves me must follow me, and where I am, there will my servant be.** (12:26)

To Preach and Exorcise

I would like to turn now to the Gospel of Mark. This Evangelist always presents the mission of Jesus beneath the twin rubric of proclaiming the Good News (his preaching and teaching), and casting out devils or exorcising. This is evident, for instance, in the opening day of his ministry in the Capernaum synagogue, where he preaches with authority, and then performs a spectacular exorcism.[27] Shortly afterwards we find a typical Marcan summary which reads:

[26] 12:24
[27] 1:21-28

And he went throughout Galilee, proclaiming the message in their synagogues and casting out demons. (1:39)

Those called to discipleship share the same mission. For Mark, discipleship means to *be with* Jesus and *to be sent out to proclaim the message, with power to cast out demons.*[28]

We may feel a little uncomfortable with the concept of exorcising. I believe that by this term Mark intends the overcoming of evil in whatever form it occurs. This can be physical, psychological, or spiritual, as seen in the story of the paralytic.[29] It can be personal, social, or institutional, as evidenced in episodes such as the healing of the leper,[30] or the woman with the severe haemorrhage.[31] Evil is present in natural phenomena like storms,[32] and religious systems like the Temple.[33] For Mark, evil is an indication that Satan still holds sway, and that the Kingdom has not yet come, that God is not yet reigning. Put in a more positive key, the mission of Jesus is to proclaim and to inaugurate the Reign of God. Through his words and deeds, the Reign of God comes near and can be experienced, bringing liberation, healing and transformation.

As disciples of Jesus we are sent to proclaim by our words, preaching, teaching, catechising, evangelising, counselling, affirming, encouraging, challenging... and by the witness of our lives and our compassion God's nearness in saving love. We are to promote and foster the values of God's Kingdom, transforming life at every level and in every sphere. Mark had this vision of a great battle between Jesus and the power of evil. We, in our day, are in the thick of this battle too, as new dimensions of evil arise amidst the old. We are called to resist and confront this evil, to work for change, to offer alternatives, to create a different world.

To Bring Good News

In Luke's Gospel, after the baptism and testing of Jesus, he returns to Galilee, *with the power of the Spirit in him*. Whatever he accomplishes in his ministry is done through the empowering Spirit. Before the summoning of any disciples he returns to his native Nazareth. It is known that he has switched from carpentry to preaching, and so he is invited to read in the synagogue on the Sabbath.

---

[28] 3:14-15
[29] 2:1-12
[30] 1:40-45
[31] 5:25-34
[32] 4:35-41

[33] 11:12-14,20; 15:38

When he came to Nazareth, where he had been brought up, he went to the synagogue on the sabbath day, as was his custom. He stood up to read, and the scroll of the prophet Isaiah was given to him. He unrolled the scroll and found the place where it was written: 'The Spirit of the Lord is upon me, because he has anointed me to bring good news to the poor. He has sent me to proclaim release to the captives and recovery of sight to the blind, to let the oppressed go free, to proclaim the year of the Lord's favour.' And he rolled up the scroll, gave it back to the attendant, and sat down. The eyes of all in the synagogue were fixed on him. Then he began to say to them, 'Today this scripture has been fulfilled in your hearing.' (Luke 4:16-21)

It appears that Jesus chooses this passage from Isaiah. He makes this prophetic dream, which encapsulates the yearnings of centuries, his own dream, his way of articulating what he is about, his manifesto or mission statement, as we would call it today. Jesus identifies himself with the one spoken of by Isaiah; he is the anointed one; the Spirit of the Lord is on him. As such he is sent to bring good news, proclaim liberty, to bring sight and freedom, to announce the Lord's year of favour. The link between Spirit and mission is expressed very closely here.

Later, when approached by two of the Baptist's disciples, asking whether he was the long-expected one, he replies:

Go and tell John what you have seen and heard: the blind receive their sight, the lame walk, the lepers are cleansed, the deaf hear, the dead are raised, the poor have good news brought to them. And blessed is anyone who takes no offence at me.
(Luke 7:22-23)

There is consistency between mission statement and realisation, dream and reality. Jesus not only preaches Good News to the poor and needy of all kinds, he *is* Good News. According to this model, this is our mission too – to be individuals and communities whose Spirit-filled presence is Good News, news which liberates, enlightens, heals and makes people glad.

PAUL AND RECONCILIATION

Paul, in his second letter to the community which he founded at Corinth, writes:

> **So if anyone is in Christ, there is a new creation: everything old has passed away; see, everything has become new! All this is from God, who reconciled us to himself through Christ, and has given us the ministry of reconciliation; that is, in Christ, God was reconciling the world to himself, not counting their trespasses against them, and entrusting the message of reconciliation to us. So we are ambassadors for Christ, since God is making his appeal through us; we entreat you on behalf of Christ, be reconciled to God.** (2 Cor 5:17-20)

This is a most beautiful extract, profoundly theological. The language of reconciliation is found in the New Testament only in Paul's writings. The term provides an alternative way than justification, redemption or salvation to describe what God has done through the death and resurrection of Jesus. At the same time it suggests yet another way of articulating Christian mission. Verses 18 and 19 are carefully balanced. In the first part of each verse the emphasis is on the initiative of God; the offer of reconciliation is God's action, God's gift. This takes place in and through Jesus Christ.

The second part of each verse focuses on the mission, the ongoing responsibility of the reconciled to proclaim what God has done and what God is offering, and so to be agents or ministers of reconciliation. Paul clearly claims that this describes his own apostolic mission, but it is applicable to other evangelists and all believers. This ministry, Paul goes on to describe as being *ambassadors of Christ*. An ambassador comes with the authority of the one sending him. The hearers, for their part, are invited to respond, to be open to the gift offered, to allow themselves to be reconciled.

In our world today there are so many situations where reconciliation is needed, not least in the land of Jesus. In families and parishes too, there is need of reconciliation, and also in religious communities. One way in which we can express our mission, is to be reconcilers, and to educate towards reconciliation.

CONCLUSION

As we become immersed in each day's activity, perhaps the recalling of some of these texts, these models, will help us to keep before our minds the overall inspiration and vision for our mission. They can be our Cathedrals. United with Jesus and empowered by the Spirit, we are sent to proclaim the Good News, to be bearers of light and revelation. We are sent to be agents of unification and unity, reconciliation and wholeness, to bring life and aliveness. We are sent to take part in the struggle to overcome all forms of evil and disunity, and to build up the Reign of God.

The Salesian Constitutions offer other ways of putting things. We are to be *deeply united with the world and its history,*[34] our pastoral activity is shaped *so as to bring about a more just world and one of greater brotherhood in Christ.*[35] And again: *Our mission is a sharing in that of the Church, which brings about the saving design of God, the coming of His Kingdom, by bringing to people the message of the Gospel, which is closely tied in with the development of the temporal order.*[36] For us too *evangelising and catechising are the fundamental characteristics of our mission.*[37]

On the inside cover of my Greek New Testament, I wrote many years ago a quotation from a French novel which I read as a student. Roughly translated it runs: *With all the power of my spirit and my heart I have wanted to be a friend, to help people live, to help them in their suffering, and to bring healing.* They are the words of a medical doctor in *Le Notaire du Havre.* I wrote them down because I thought at the time that they said a lot to me about Jesus, and summed up what, in my youthful idealism, I wanted my life to be. A few years ago I celebrated my silver jubilee of ordination, and reflected a great deal on these words. In today's jargon they would probably amount to a personal mission statement. I think I still try to stand by them. Luke, as we have seen, has Jesus quote Isaiah in the Nazareth synagogue at the start of his ministry. The words are like a manifesto, articulating how Jesus saw his ministry and mission. If you haven't done so already, why not try to spell out your personal truth in a few telling phrases, the way you see your life mission today, at this stage in your journey of discipleship.

80

34 Constitution 7
35 Constitution 7
36 Constitution 31
37 Constitution 34

PRAYER SUGGESTION

We could ask whether we see ourselves as people who are *sent*, who have an important mission in life. We could also see which of the models of mission we have been considering excites and energises us. We could ponder our own personal mission statement, and work out its practical implications.

CHAPTER NINE - EMMAUS

The Emmaus story is one of the most beautiful narratives in the New Testament, and, according to some, perhaps even in world literature. It is an exquisite masterpiece in which Luke's theological and artistic talents are seen at their finest, a literary gem. It takes up again the themes of the journey and the meal, themes prominent in Luke's telling of the Gospel story. In recent years Salesians have looked to this story for inspiration when reflecting on their ministry of accompaniment on the journey of faith. In this chapter I suggest that we ponder the narrative primarily as God's word to ourselves on our own journey; only then can it also become a model for ministry.

In the various Gospels there are several resurrection appearance narratives, and they tend to have a number of common features, rather like a basic template or pattern. The Emmaus narrative is no exception.

- a situation is described in which the disciples, bereft of the Master, are despondent and disappointed and fearful;

- Jesus suddenly becomes present;

- there is some form of greeting by Jesus, and a period of hesitancy or doubt and non-recognition on the part of the disciples;

- the climactic moment of recognition;

- finally, Jesus sends them forth on mission.

This scheme provides a useful framework for our reflections.

THE BEREFT SITUATION

The story begins on the first day of the week. The two disciples are making their way home after the Passover festival to the village of Emmaus, about seven miles from Jerusalem. Some scholars suggest that they may be man and wife, if

Cleopas is the same person as the Clopas of John's version of the Calvary scene.[1] As they walk along leaden-footed, they share the depths of their distress and disappointment. As so often happens in situations of grief and bereavement, they recall what has taken place, retrace familiar contours, in an attempt to keep the person alive, clinging in tight-gripped desperation to a past which had meaning and which brought joy and love. We sense the tragedy and poignancy of their situation, the pained brokenness of shattered dreams, articulated later in the story: *Our hope had been that he would be the one to set Israel free.* We detect the tones of anguish, bitterness and near despair, and glimpse the empty void which is their future.

A significant factor in the setting is that the two disciples are on their way from Jerusalem. A salient feature of Luke's presentation of the ministry of Jesus is his structural emphasis on Jesus' journey up to Jerusalem, clearly inaugurated in the words:

> **When the days drew near for him to be taken up, he set his face to go to Jerusalem.** (9:51)

It is there that the events of his death and resurrection take place. It is there that the gift of the Spirit will be bestowed. It is from that city that the apostles will set forth on mission to the nations. Yet these disciples are walking away; they have turned their backs; they have thrown in the towel; they have abandoned their friends. As we learn later, they have even heard the women's tale of the empty tomb and angelic vision with its Easter proclamation - but they are walking away in grief and unbelief, hopes shattered, expectations in pieces.

THE APPEARANCE OF JESUS

Then, suddenly, a stranger is walking with them, as the Risen Jesus takes the initiative and breaks through, unannounced and unexpected, into the shredded web of their lives and into the midst of their tragedy. He walks with them along the twisting, dusty road. They avidly seize on his ignorance, and capitalise on the opportunity to tell their story all over again. He listens to their words and to their *angst*, listens with compassion and understanding. He lives with them their questioning bewilderment. He is content to wait, prompting them with a question or two to enable them to bring out their problem, not forcing the pace, not rushing in with instant solutions. He walks their way with them, stopping and starting with their halting rhythm.

[1] Jn 19:25

FAILURE TO RECOGNISE JESUS

But the two disciples fail to recognise him, in accordance with the normal pattern in resurrection narratives; and their failure is protracted. *Something kept them from seeing who it was.* This motif of non-recognition is one of the devices by which the Evangelists underline the *otherness* of Jesus, the radical transformation which has taken place. Its persistence in this story adds considerably to the dramatic effect. It also serves to illustrate the truth that vision of the Risen One is not a human achievement. It is gift, God's gift.

At this point in the unfolding of the story, Luke very skilfully, and not without a touch of irony, puts on the lips of Cleopas a summary of the early Christian kerygma (similar to the preaching of Peter and Paul).[2] Jesus is described in terms of the popular estimate of him as *a prophet mighty in deed and word before God and all the people.* A brief résumé of the Passion follows, with emphasis on the responsibility of the Jewish leaders. Cleopas goes on to express the hopes which Jesus had aroused in their own hearts. He was, in fact, the prophet, the prophet-like-Moses, the liberator of his people. However their hopes had been dashed by his untimely death. Finally, he mentions the empty tomb: the women's visit, the absence of the body, the astounding angelic vision and proclamation, the journey to the tomb made by some of the disciples in search of corroboration as hope was rekindled and as suddenly snuffed out in scepticism.

Jesus then responds, jolting them initially with a reproach for their failure to understand God's ways. From the scriptures he provides the key to the recent events:

Was it not necessary that the Messiah should suffer these things and then enter into his glory? (24:26)

Jesus leads them through the Bible, highlighting the evidence of God's purpose, detecting an underlying common pattern in God's ways. This was a foreshadowing of the pattern of his own mission: rejection leading to acceptance, suffering leading to glory. Pre-Christian Judaism does not seem to have widely expected a suffering Messiah. That was why the idea of the cross was such a scandal to the disciples, and the early Christian preaching of a crucified Messiah such an absurdity for Jewish ears. The first Christians combed

[2] Acts 2:22-24 and 13:26f.

the scriptures to seek enlightenment, both to clarify and underpin their own faith and to support their preaching. Jesus shows them that not only is suffering not incompatible with messianic kingship; it is God's providential pathway to glory.

RECOGNITION

So enthralled and absorbed are they in the conversation that the miles imperceptibly slip by, and suddenly Jesus and the two disciples find themselves on the outskirts of Emmaus village, probably the couple's home. The two are no longer so self-absorbed; they feel concern for the stranger's need. Jesus makes as if to go on, a gesture which evokes that beautiful invitation:

> **Stay with us, because it is almost evening and the day is now nearly over.** (24:29)

It is not without significance that Jesus waits to be asked, for he never imposes himself, never forces his friendship; with remarkable sensitivity he reverences our freedom. But once the offer of hospitality is extended, he accepts promptly.[3] Later they sit at table together. Jesus, though the guest, assumes the role of host:

> **He took bread, blessed and broke it, and gave it to them.** (24:30)

As has happened so often in the ministry, as Luke tells the story, we find Jesus eating with broken people. He reaches out and touches them in their failure and disloyalty, their fragility and inadequacy. He breaks with them the bread of reconciliation and friendship. That outreach and acceptance in table fellowship transforms their understanding and opens their eyes, and at last they recognise him. At this, he vanishes from their midst.

COMMISSIONING

The Emmaus narrative does not conform precisely to the pattern of appearance stories in its conclusion, for there is no explicit commissioning. Nevertheless, the sense of mission is strongly in evidence, for the effect of the encounter with the Lord is that the disciples depart without delay in spite of impending darkness. They retrace their route to Jerusalem in order to reach out and share

---

3 see also Rev 3:20; John 14:23

with the others of their band this gladdening news so filled with promise. Having abandoned Jerusalem in disappointment and scepticism, they now return in faith, with a spring in their step and a smile in their eyes, their hearts on fire, to begin afresh. *Where before they were ex-followers of a dead prophet, now they are followers of the Risen Lord.*4 On their arrival, the two disciples find the eleven and the rest of the company assembled, and their news is confirmed:

The Lord has risen indeed, and he has appeared to Simon! (24:34)

The Risen Jesus has reached out to Simon in a similar way, extending to him too his forgiveness and fellowship. As the whole company talk together excitedly about these extraordinary occurrences, Jesus suddenly appears in their midst, and they share a meal of fish (and bread, presumably). Their fellowship is re-established and renewed, a fellowship which then erupts into mission, as Jesus sends them to proclaim to all nations, the Good News of repentance and forgiveness. Good News which they have experienced so profoundly in table fellowship with him.

REFLECTIONS

This narrative is such a rich source for our reflection. In fact, I believe that it can be said that the Evangelist is less concerned with the resurrection of Jesus as a past event than with the active presence of the Risen Lord in the life of the community. He is interested in highlighting those aspects and areas of our living where Jesus continues to encounter us today.

Firstly, it is so easy for us to empathise with the Emmaus couple in their loss and bereavement experience, and in their need to talk about their dreams and their pain and disillusionment. We have been there too. At times our schemes and dreams and plans fall apart. It is a struggle to see meaning in failure or change, oppression or injustice, in loss of any kind. We can feel let down by friends, by people in leadership roles, by those we seek to serve and to whom we minister, by our family, the Church, by God. There can be much anger and frustration and hurt within us. Luke is assuring us that Jesus is present with us in these situations, in our stumbles and struggles, when we feel *let down*. He is walking our way alongside us as faithful companion and friend. It is so important to acknowledge our pain, and to share our feelings with him in our prayer, to allow

4 D McBride, *Luke*, p 320

him into our messiness and shadows. His strengthening and liberating presence is frequently mediated by others, fellow travellers, who, through their own suffering and journeying, have learned how to *be with*. They have learned how to listen, empathise, offer a healing space and hospitality. It is important to be able to trust, and share our disappointment. Some people carry this kind of pain for years and years. It can affect and infect relationships, decisions, attitudes, ministry.

Secondly, the failure of the disciples to recognise Jesus can stimulate us to ask what it is in ourselves which can hinder the realisation of his presence with us. The disciples seem too depressed, too caught up in their problems and grief. Perhaps their God is too small, their expectations too limited and narrow. They are not open to what is new and unexpected and freely given, to a God of such unfathomable love. We, too, can at times be bogged down in the rut of routine, or the heavy sands of our problems and preoccupations; we can be just too busy. We can be blinded by our self-centredness or introspection, deafened by the strident sounds inside and around us. Perhaps we are looking for a God fashioned to our own sketchy design; perhaps we are pining for what is tried and comfortable, afraid of letting go, of losing our control and security. Like the Emmaus couple, we can thus be closed to the divine stranger, and he goes unrecognised.

Thirdly, one of the points which the Evangelist wishes to teach us through this narrative is that in the study and prayerful pondering of scripture the Risen Lord is to be encountered. He is reassuringly present, deepening our insight and understanding, widening our perspectives, firming up our commitment, disturbing and challenging our lives, *setting our hearts on fire*. The Risen Jesus is present whenever his life-giving word is proclaimed, the Good News of God's forgiveness, acceptance, and faithful love. It is a word which also summons us to model our lives on the messianic pattern of his, and to surrender in trust to the mystery of God's loving plan. Today there is much greater interest in reflecting on scripture. It's worth asking ourselves whether we are indeed people of the word.

Fourthly, one of the details of the narrative which fascinates me is the change which takes place in the disciples as they listen to Jesus' words. As long as they are concerned exclusively with their own problems and grief and disappointment, their horizons are shrouded in thick cloud. But their focus changes; they begin to look beyond themselves; they see the stranger's need for food and shelter and rest; they open their hearts to the other. The clouds then begin to lift and the sun filters through. In this, I believe that the Evangelist is reminding us that the Risen Lord is present and can be encountered wherever there is care and service of others, however ordinary and prosaic its mode of expression might be. Selflessness can open our eyes so that we may catch a glimpse of him. I think that it is also true that our love, hospitality and acceptance of others can be the occasion for them to perceive that he is touching their lives too.

Fifthly, for the two disciples, recognition finally takes place at table in the breaking of bread. Luke is reminding us that it is in the eucharist that the presence of the Risen Lord continues in the Christian community; in the eucharistic celebration, *the central act of every Salesian community*,[5] he can be encountered most powerfully in our midst. We celebrate the eucharist repeatedly as fragile and imperfect disciples. Eucharist is a reconciling event. It is an encounter with the Risen Jesus which has the potential to transform and reshape our lives. I find this element particularly moving and meaningful.

Finally, beyond this narrative, I think that it would be true to say that Luke would have us know that the Risen Lord is with us as we reach out in mission, *preaching repentance for the forgiveness of sins to all nations*, particularly through the gift of the Spirit. The book of Acts bears eloquent and persuasive witness to this.

CONCLUSION

As we move forward into our future, I believe that it is important that we take with us the message of Luke in this profound Emmaus narrative. Our lives will also be much richer if we can become more aware of the many areas of everyday experience which can serve as pointers to the meaning of resurrection:

- peace after conflict,

- calm after storm,

- fresh stream water on aching feet,

5 Constitution 88.

- the snowdrops and daffodils of spring after long, grey winters,

- success after failure and disappointment,

- reunion after separation or estrangement,

- relief from tension and anxiety and depression,

- cure from illness and infirmity,

- liberation from any form of slavery.

In short, any death situation transformed into a situation of newness, life and promise.

If we reflected a little more, we would, I'm sure, discover that our lives are shot through with rays of resurrection light, moments and events which help us to understand a little more what is meant by the Easter proclamation *He is risen*. The promise this holds for us is the source of Salesian joy and optimism. We would become more sensitive to his presence with us on our journey, and better prepared to encounter him when he comes in forgiveness and fellowship, in word and sacrament. We all have Emmaus moments. Perhaps they are not quite so dramatic, but they are no less real and transforming.

In the light of reflection on our own experience, we shall, I believe, find this narrative an exciting model for ministry as we journey with the young people and others entrusted to our care. We are called to walk alongside them, even when they are travelling in the wrong direction! We are to be present with them, accepting them where they are, listening to their story, feeling their hopes and their disappointments. We move at their pace, respecting their dignity and freedom. There is perhaps a time to ask a question, a time to suggest an explanation, a time to offer a challenge, a time to share our experience too. We can accept and offer hospitality, and share *table fellowship*. We seek together to become aware of the Risen One present in our lives. We can involve them more creatively in reaching out to others in friendship and service, with a twinkle of joy in their eyes and hope in their step. We may break together the bread of Word and sacrament, and forge together new ways of responding to the Gospel of Jesus. Together we may experience new Emmaus moments, and, our hearts burning within us, find our way to a new Jerusalem, a place where we have never been before.

PRAYER SUGGESTION

We might reflect on the different stages of the Emmaus story, and be sensitive to the way these resonate with our own *ordinary* experience. We could also recall Emmaus moments in our own life. We could ask ourselves how the Emmaus narrative can serve as a model for our own relationships and ministry.